THE
REST
OF
GRACE

WAYNE BARBER

HARVEST HOUSE PUBLISHERS
Eugene, Oregon 97042

Except where otherwise indicated, all Scripture quotations in this book are taken from the New American Standard Bible, © 1960, 1962, 1963, 1968, 1971, 1972, 1973, 1975, 1977 by The Lockman Foundation. Used by permission.

Cover by Left Coast Design, Portland, Oregon

THE REST OF GRACE
Copyright © 1998 by Wayne Barber
Published by Harvest House Publishers
Eugene, Oregon 97402

Library of Congress Cataloging-in-Publication Data

Barber, Wayne, 1953–
    The rest of grace   /   Wayne Barber and Chip MacGregor.
      p. cm.
    ISBN 1-56507-944-2
    1. Christian life.   I. MacGregor, Chip, 1958-   II. Title.
BV4501.2.B38274   1998
248.4—dc21   98-6164
                                             CIP

Printed in the United States of America.

     98 99 00 01 02 03 / BP / 10 9 8 7 6 5 4 3 2 1

This book is dedicated to my precious family:
to my wife, who truly is my best friend and has been
for 29 years; to my precious daughter, who causes the
sun to come up when she walks into a room; to my son,
whose smile, friendship, and wonderful personality
minister to me constantly; to my son-in-law, who far
surpasses anything I could ever have wanted in a
son-in-law; and of course to "little bit,"
little Hollen, my granddaughter, a precious jewel
who is my partner in having a good time.

—Wayne Barber

For Vic Walter,
who taught me the truth
of Robert Murray McCheyne:
"A holy minister is an
awful weapon in the hand of God."

—Chip MacGregor

Acknowledgments

I would like to acknowledge several people that God has used greatly in my Christian life. I wish to thank:

Dr. Spiros Zodhiates, of AMG International, my dear friend and mentor, for the years he has invested in my life trying to teach a true hard head the Greek language.

Jack and Kay Arthur, of Precept Ministries, for their willingness to allow me to be a part of the greatest Bible study I've ever known for teaching people how to get into the Word of God.

Roy Hession, author of *The Calvary Road,* for being the vessel God used to start my journey in learning the Christ-life. Brother Roy taught me how to go to the cross daily and to always "take the low road."

Ian Thomas, author of *The Saving Life of Christ,* for teaching me how to walk "from the cross," with Jesus being Jesus in me.

Manley Beasley, who is in heaven now, for being the vessel that God used to teach me the beauty of living by faith alone.

Dr. Bill Stafford, evangelist and dear friend, for being the vessel God used to teach me what it means to "give" and to "get," and for being such an encouragement in my life.

Ron Dunn, teacher, author, preacher, and friend, for being the vessel God used to teach me how to walk through the valleys of life knowing that God is and always will be in control.

Chip MacGregor, for helping me create this book.

The people of *Woodland Park Baptist Church,* for allowing me the freedom to be what God has called me to be, and loving me in the process.

Most of all, I thank my God, who loved me long before I ever knew Him and came to die for me on the cross. I thank Him for His shed blood, but I also thank Him for His shared life! As you can see, when I stand before God one day, if there are any crowns in heaven for me, I will have to give them to others whom God has used in my life to help me get to where I am before we take them all and lay them at the precious feet of Jesus.

Contents

❧

❧

Experiencing the Rest of Grace

Not long ago I was working on a jigsaw puzzle that has more than a thousand little pieces. For long hours I sat trying to fit them together in various ways, sorting according to color or shape or design, and watching it slowly come together. There is a sense of urgency and accomplishment that drives me as I see the various elements begin to form a whole, and I felt I was nearing the finish when something occurred to me: A piece was missing. When I finally got all the pieces together, I felt disappointment rather than completion. No puzzle is complete unless *all* the pieces come together.

The funny thing is, that feeling best describes how I used to feel about my Christian walk. There was a piece missing. I tried with all the energy I could to do the right thing, but I could never quite achieve it. I tried loving people, only to be driven away from them. I tried gritting my teeth and getting through tough times in my own strength, only to end up facing failure and frustration. I searched the Scriptures, but there was something missing in my spiritual walk.

Then one day, through the grace of God's Word, it hit me: *I was still trying to do it myself.* I was trying to be a "good" Christian, trying to force myself to do things I hate, and trying to accomplish things in my own power. In essence, I was still trying to save myself. My striving was of the flesh, and as I read my Bible it dawned on me that was the very reason God had sent His Spirit into my life—to give me rest from my own fleshly striving. Christ didn't just give me life, He *is* my life. He empowers me to do what He knows I cannot do without Him.

In Matthew 11:28-30, Jesus says, "Come unto Me, all who are weary and heavy laden, and I will give you rest. Take my yoke upon you, and learn from Me, for I am gentle and humble in heart; and you shall find *rest* for your souls. For My yoke is easy, and My load is light." Here I had been trying to do the work myself, and Jesus was telling me to rest in Him. I had been trying to achieve spiritual greatness through my own power, and the Lord was saying it could only be found in Him.

That's the message of grace. When we learn that Christ is our life, we can *rest* in His grace. Imagine that for a moment: allowing yourself to experience the rest of grace. That's what I did . . . and that message changed my life.

Now when I face the valley of discouragement, I am quickly reminded of the message of grace. I still have a responsibility, but it is to run to the cross and confess my inability rather than to tough it out and attack life's struggles in my own power. Through surrender to Jesus, I have learned to enter into the wonder of the life He gave me. His grace empowers and comforts me, allowing me to understand that He is truly in control.

If you have been striving and looking for something more in your spiritual walk, you need to read this book. I want you to experience the rest of grace. This book won't resolve every issue you face—it's not intended to be the answer to every possible problem. But if it can help you recover that missing piece to your Christian life, the fact that Christ is your life, and you need nothing else, then it can be used of God in a mighty way. My prayer is that you'll let the joy of His power give you the rest you've been seeking.

— *Wayne Barber*
Chattanooga, Tennessee

What's Wrong with Me?

Every morning my daughter Stephanie would get up at 6:00 A.M. to get ready for school, and soon would be brushing her hair. At 6:15 she was brushing her hair. At 6:30 she was still brushing her hair. At 7:00 I would go by the bathroom door and say, "Now, Stephanie, remember we're going to leave at 8:00 A.M. to go to school."

"I hear you, daddy," she would holler back as she continued to brush her hair.

By about 7:30 her hair would begin to frizz from the stroking. She would not be able to do anything with it.

Finally, I would go by the door at 7:50 and say, "Stephanie, we have got to go!"

"I hear you, daddy!" would come the reply, shouted through the bathroom door.

So my son and I would go out to the car and wait. We got to know each other very well during those days while we were waiting for Stephanie to get ready for school. Each morning my daughter would come racing out to the car at the last minute, hair flying off into space, a frustrated look on her face. She would often have something profound to say to us, touching on the unfairness of life, the mysteries of the universe, and the hair she inherited from my side of the family.

One particular morning as Stephanie was coming around the corner of the house to get to the car, she slipped and fell on an icy sidewalk. I didn't see her fall, but I saw the results of it—books flying, feet in the air, steam rising from her ears. Before she could reach us I told my son, "This is going to be good today, son, so pay attention."

Stephanie got in the car and slammed the door, her ripped hose increasing her frustration level by the second. Her composure was absolutely gone.

"Good morning, Stephanie," I said sweetly.

"Daddy," she muttered, lips pressed tightly together, "I've got something to tell you."

"What's that, dear?"

"I don't care what you preach, I don't care what you think, I don't care what the Bible teaches—*there is no way you can live the Christian life!*"

I drove in silence for moment, smiling to myself. "Well, thank you, Stephanie. I'll try my best to encourage somebody with that wonderful truth today." Steven just sat in the back seat grinning.

We got halfway to school when the Holy Spirit began to minister to my heart. "Wait a minute—what did she just say?" I wondered to myself. *There is no way you can live the Christian life.* The more I reflected on her words, the more impressed I became.

When we pulled into the school parking lot, I turned to my daughter, took her arm gently, and said, "Stephanie, remember what you said? That you can't live the Christian life?"

"Yeah. At least that's how I feel."

"Well, honey, I want you to know something: *You're exactly right.*"

She looked at me for a moment, wondering what I was saying.

"Where in Scripture does it ever say we can live the Christian life?" I asked her. "It doesn't. You're absolutely right, Stephanie. You cannot live it." I let her think about that for a minute before adding, "*You* can't, but Christ can live it in you." Then I gave her a peck on the cheek and sent my daughter on her way.

Christ Is Our Life

The more I've had a chance to meditate on my daughter's frustrated words, the more I believe them. We simply can't live the Christian life. We try and try. We read books about how to achieve it, we go to seminars that claim to reveal the secrets, and we listen to preachers tell us how to get to the next step in our faith, but we never quite get there. The fact is, *we can't live the Christian life*, so we have to let Christ live it in us.

Christ is our life. He didn't just give us life; He *is* our life. As we learn to let Christ be in us what we are not, the Christian life begins to take place in us. That to me is the basis of my entire ministry. It is also the message of this book. *Jesus Christ died to set us free from our old patterns of frustration and failure. He wants to live life through us, giving us a whole new way to live.*

A lot of believers are frustrated because they have grown up in the church and have heard all these messages about how they ought to live. They've read their daily devotionals every day. Maybe they've participated in a Bible study or joined a small group. They go to church Sunday morning and Sunday evening. If they're really spiritual they go on Wednesday night to prayer meeting. They keep trying to find the key to the happy, fulfilled spiritual life that's talked about in Scripture. But the feeling they're left with is that something is missing.

Something isn't quite right about their lives even though they have heard the preacher talk about the fulfilled life. They've heard spiritual people talk about this wonderful walk with Christ, and they've read about it in books. Yet they feel as if that special "something" that should be there is missing.

I'm not saying these people are not Christians. They love the Lord, and they are on their way to glory. But at the same time they have a feeling of frustration with their Christian walk.

When someone comes to me and says, "Wayne, I'm frustrated with the Christian life. I just can't live it. What should I do?" I say to him, "My friend, you are in a great spot!" Frustration is simply a symptom of a person trying to do what he cannot do. When he gets to the end of himself, he begins to realize that there must be more to it than he thought.

A frustrated believer is in a wonderful place, because he or she is ready to discover the truth about living like Jesus Christ: He can't do it on his own. Once he realizes this truth, he is ready to hear the good news that Christ can start to live through him.

It's like someone who says, "I'm going to get up tomorrow, and I'm going to live for Jesus. God loves everybody, so I'm going to love everybody." By nine in the morning God puts a brother in his life who is hard to love. By noon he is already frustrated with his inability to love his brother. He cries out, "Lord, I can't!" And Christ replies back to him, "I never said you could. That's why I came to live in you. That's why I *am* your life."

To me, the frustration comes when I don't realize the sinful potential of the flesh that I have to live with until Jesus comes back. As Christians we need to realize that the flesh was a problem before we got saved, and it is also a problem *after* we get saved. We are going to have to learn to deal with our flesh *daily* in order to experience the things that God has for us. So we can expect frustration in the Christian life.

A lady came to me one day and said, "You know, since I've gotten saved, all hell has broken loose." I said to her, "Welcome to the normal Christian life! What did you expect? Christ didn't call you to a party—He called you into a battle. Now the war starts." You see, many Christians want to rejoice that they've been saved *from* something. They've been saved from their past, saved from their mistakes, saved from their sins.

But we've also been saved *to* something, and Christ wants us living for Him in the daily battle. Our battle is not only with the devil, but also with the flesh and with ourselves. The beautiful thing about salvation is that I've been saved from self. Wayne Barber has been saved from Wayne. I've been saved from something, but I've also been saved *to* something—a new life in Jesus Christ.

The Bible talks about the church as being the *ekklesia*, the "called out ones." As a believer, I've been called out of my old life into a brand-new way of living. I have to learn to completely rethink how I live. Romans 12:1,2 says, "I urge you therefore, brethren, by the mercies of God, to present your bodies a living and holy sacrifice, acceptable to God, which is your spiritual service of worship. And do not be conformed to this world, but be transformed by the renewing of your mind, that you may prove what the will of God is, that which is good and acceptable and perfect." I have to learn to think differently now that I am a brand-new creature. I have to learn to think God's way. The frustration for many Christians comes after being saved but still trying to do things the way they used to do them—in their own strength.

No Longer the Same

In Romans chapters 6 and 7 the apostle Paul showed the Roman believers that they were new creatures: "For if we have become united with Him in the likeness of His death, certainly we shall be also in the likeness of His resurrection" (Romans 6:5). The word *united* is an intimate word. It means to be blended together, much like a baker blends the various ingredients together in order to create something new. Christ's life has been "baked" into us, if you will. That's why I like telling people in churches that we are "biscuits" for Jesus.

Paul continues by telling the Romans, "...knowing this, that our old self was crucified with Him, that our body of sin might be done away with, that we should no longer be slaves to sin" (Romans 6:6). The old man is dead. What I was in Adam I can never be again. The Spirit of God has come to live in me and has made me a brand-new creature. I can never be like I was in Adam. When Paul says, "that our body of sin might be done away with," the actual idea is that the body has been rendered powerless. The word in Greek means "destroyed." The power of sin in me is destroyed completely.

But if the power of sin is destroyed, why do we still sin? Because we continue living in these corrupt bodies, even though in the eyes of God we are holy. Think of it as a car being shifted into neutral. You can have the most expensive automobile on the road, but as long as you keep it in neutral, you won't be going anywhere. When our flesh is in neutral, there is no power to do anything sinful. However, it did not cease to exist. The transmission did not fall out. If I choose to shift it back into gear by my choosing to sin, then my flesh can come back and control me.

When the average Christian first gets saved, he does not realize the truth of this principle. Instead, he tries to overcome the drive to sin by redirecting its power to some other area. For example, he may become extremely religious to compensate for his failure. But Paul says in Romans 7:9, "I was once alive apart from the Law; but when the commandment came, sin became alive, and I died." Ask yourself a question: When was Paul ever alive without the law? When he didn't yet fully understand the grace of God. Until that time, he was *physically* alive, but he was trying to develop a relationship with God through his own good works. Once we are saved, most of us want to continue seeking the Lord through our works, since we don't know any other way.

The law demands that my flesh act. My flesh *wants* to act. In other words, the law demands works. My flesh responds to that by seeking to work. The problem is that what the law demands it also condemns. Everything I do in the energy of my flesh the law is going to condemn. That's the frustration of a person who is trying to be saved by his own works. He can't do it. That is also the frustration of a person who is saved and is trying to live the Christian life by his own works. He can't do it either. To overcome this frustration, he'll try shifting his energy into some other law. He may attempt to impose the "Quiet Time" law or the "Be Like Jesus" law. He'll seek some external way to work toward salvation. However we define "the flesh," this we know: The flesh loves the law.

Because sin takes opportunity through the commandments (Romans 7:8), the commandments become a base of operations for sin to work. Therefore my flesh tries to work. When Paul says, "I once was alive apart from the Law" (Romans 7:9), I believe he is talking about a time just after his Damascus road salvation experience. Once he got saved, the Lord had to teach him a new way to live. Many years are missing in Paul's life and many believe that several years were spent in the desert, where the Holy Spirit taught him about grace. However, when he came back among his peers, suddenly it dawned on Paul that he was getting back into the old mindset. It occurred to him that even though he was saved, his religious flesh was still as powerful as it had ever been. He could still put himself back under law. Paul realized that something had to conquer his desire to be under law. Something had to set him free from his old way of living. That's when he says in Romans 7:24b, "Who will set me free from the body of this death?" His answer in Romans 7:25 is clear: "Thanks be to God through Jesus Christ our Lord!"

Sanctified by Christ

Read through Romans chapter 7 sometime, and you'll see how frustrated Paul could get over his sin. In essence he says, "I try and I try, and I can't do it. Things that I want to do I can't. Things that I don't want to do I keep doing." Everywhere I go, I see that this is the frustration the average Christian is feeling. Everybody can identify with Paul.

A friend of mine was in a Bible study one time, and as they were sitting in a circle in his living room, one of the men was asked to read Romans 7 out loud. His wife was standing in the kitchen talking to my friend's wife. When this man's wife heard him, she came into the room to see what was going on. She thought he was telling his own story! The words of Paul were exactly what he had been expressing to her the day before. She thought her husband was talking from the heart, telling the group what he was experiencing in his Christian life.

How many Christians feel defeated and totally frustrated because they are trying to live the Christian life in their own power? I would guess the answer is "most of them." Perfection (or some magical spiritual formula) is always a goal that people try to attain but can't. If they put themselves under "the law" of being like Jesus, they will never do it. If they put themselves under "the law" of having a quiet time every morning at 4:00 A.M. in hopes that their day will go better, it won't work. We have to learn to live under grace, for *we are not under law.*

Many people think that in Romans 7:14-25 the person Paul is talking about is not a Christian. They think that Paul is either writing about a time prior to his own salvation experience or else talking about somebody else. To me that doesn't fit Paul's argument, for in Romans 7:14 he says, "For we know that the Law is spiritual; but I am of flesh, sold into bondage to sin." That verse reveals the reality of Paul's first-person situation. Paul says that his *flesh* is still *devoted to sin.* Our flesh is always going to be devoted to sin, and I think Paul came to that same realization. That's why he says, "For what I am doing I do not understand." In Romans 7:17 he adds, "So now, no longer am I the one doing it, but sin which indwells me." In other words, Paul understood the principle of sin dwelling in his flesh.

I love the last part of that chapter, in which he writes, "Wretched man that I am! Who will set me free from the body of this death? Thanks be to God through Jesus Christ our Lord!" (Romans 7:24,25). The One who has saved Paul is the One who will sanctify him. Paul can't sanctify himself—that is, he cannot make himself holy. That's the trap Christians fall into. We try to clean ourselves up so that we appear holy to people. We quit smoking, or stop going to movies, and think that by abandoning a few behaviors we have made ourselves "better."

Believers who try to make themselves holy by "not doing this" or "not doing that" have missed the point. The Christian life is not a matter of stopping some things or starting others. Our ability to sin or not to sin is a result of the Holy Spirit living in us and leading us to be like Him. The Lord separates us as we cooperate with Him.

We Can't, But He Can

In Romans 8:1 Paul tells us, "There is therefore now no condemnation for those who are in Christ Jesus." Many Christians would say the same things that Paul said in Romans 7:14-25 and then conclude that they are not even saved. But not the apostle. Paul says, "There is no condemnation for Christians." If you've given your life to Him, everything has changed! You will still have the same battles Paul had, and struggle with fleshly temptations, but now Christ is in you so that you don't fight those battles alone.

I am encouraged that the apostle Paul struggled with the same things I struggle with. His flesh was no different than mine. It's one of the few things I have in common with Paul! I think Christians often tend to deify the apostles and the prophets; however, they were just ordinary people like you and I are. The fact that they had struggles encourages me. I look to see where they found their answers, and I realize that where they found their answers is the same place I can find answers. Paul had to keep dying to his flesh. He had to say no to what the flesh wanted by learning to say yes to Christ and then letting the Holy Spirit take command of his life. Then he became the vessel through which Christ could do His work. That's the whole key: *Christ lived His life through Paul.* It was not Paul living like Jesus and trying to do things for Him, but it was Christ living through Paul. That is the key to living the Christian life.

That's why I call this principle "the Christ life." We have to realize that *we can't,* but *He can.* Galatians 2:20 says, "I am crucified with Christ; and it is no longer I who live, but Christ lives in me." It is *His* life living in me.

If I hold up my coat and say, "Sleeve, raise yourself," that sleeve will not do anything. There is no life in the coat to enable it to do what it needs to do. But when I put that coat on and say, "Sleeve, raise yourself," then the sleeve rises up—not because of the coat, but because of the life that is *in* the coat. That is exactly what Paul is saying in the book of Romans—our lives are like empty sleeves, and Christ fills them. It is Christ who is living in me.

Think about the words Paul used to describe a believer's life in Christ:

- "For I am confident of this very thing, that He who began a good work in you will perfect it until the day of Christ Jesus" (Philippians 1:6).

- "For to me, to live is Christ and to die is gain" (Philippians 1:21).

- "When Christ, who is our life, is revealed, then you also will be revealed with Him in glory" (Colossians 3:4).

These statements form a foundation for understanding grace as a product of our new birth in Christ. He lives in us to enable us to do what He has commanded us to do. Previously I was under the law and condemned by it, but now I'm no longer under the law. I'm under grace. Christ lives in me. He enables me to do what He has commanded me to do. A believer has to grasp this concept if he is to ever become mature in the Lord. He has to come to the end of himself and start realizing what he *can't* do before he can grasp what God *can* do in and through him. This book isn't just another step-by-step process that promises instant maturity, but an encouragement for believers to see their relationship with the Lord in a new way.

The Christ life is not merely trying some new plan for spiritual growth; it is learning to live out of His power. It is learning to appropriate the power of God and put it to use for His glory.

Learning to Find Victory

I don't know how many times on a Sunday morning I have studied my Bible and prayed, prepared myself for living the Christian life, and seen it all go up in smoke within 20 minutes. I'll get in my car, drive about two miles, and discover that idiots have taken over the interstate. They will not even allow me to get *on* the interstate! I'll try everything I can to get on, but people won't get over in the passing lane or slow down in order to let me share the road. Once I do get on, I'll sit behind some old bird who thinks it's dangerous to go over 35 miles per hour. And all the time I'm being passed by drivers who have mistaken our Tennessee highways for the Indianapolis 500. By the time I get two miles down the road, I've forgotten all about living the Christian life. Instead, I'm ready to run over somebody on the interstate. But when I pull into the church parking lot it dawns on me: "You're going to preach." I realize anew how wicked my flesh really is, how subtle is the temptation of the flesh. I have to end up confessing and dying to my flesh, asking God to forgive me of my sin before I can stand up in the pulpit and preach.

My failure shows me every day what I *can't* do. Over and over again I am reminded that I can't live the Christian life in my own power. God is faithful to orchestrate circumstances in my life and drive me to the point of understanding what I cannot accomplish on my own. The Christian who is frustrated needs to read this book and get a new perspective on what "living for Jesus" is all about.

The Good News of Christ is not just getting people saved. Paul wrote to the Christians in Rome, "Thus, for my part, I am eager to preach the gospel to you also who are in Rome" (Romans 1:15). Why would he want to preach the gospel to the Christians? Don't we preach the gospel just to the lost? Paul had grown in his knowledge of God, and longed to share his new life in Christ with those believers.

The Good News is that Christ did not just give me life. Christ *is* my life. I've got to remember that, and if I don't, I don't understand what the Good News really is. In Ephesians 6:15 Paul says, "...having shod your feet with the preparation of the gospel of peace." Everybody thinks this verse is talking about how to get people saved, but it isn't. Paul is reminding us that to become strong in the faith and ready for battle, we have to keep our feet firmly planted in the truth of the gospel. We must have a solid grasp of what the Good News really is. The Good News, as I read it in the Bible, is simply the truth about how we can live in the victory of Christ's life. Too many Christians feel saved, but have no victory. Peace comes as they feel secure in knowing the Lord lives in them and wants to live through them. So let's explore what takes our peace away, then examine how we can move away from frustration and toward peace and security in Christ.

Addicted to Sin

One of the problems most Christians have is not realizing how quickly sin can overtake them. For example, I own a computer. One day my son warned me, "Dad, be careful of what is on that computer."

"What do you mean, Steven?"

"Well, it's like an encyclopedia. You can get anything you want off it."

Here I am a 54-year-old man, staring at this plastic box full of wires and plastic parts. I look at my computer and think, "Is he really telling the truth?"

So that afternoon I decided to try out the Internet. I typed in one word, and immediately my computer shifted into a different gear. Suddenly, before my eyes my computer screen was filled with things that I hadn't even imagined could be on there. That's when it dawned on me: "Barber, the flesh is one wicked thing." As a believer, I don't want to be ruled by my flesh, so I have to learn to reckon with it. The flesh will quickly take mastery over me if I am not able to understand the principle of grace.

Grace is God's enabling me to turn off my flesh. Grace is His enabling me to overcome sin. But *I* can't overcome it. If I try, it will overcome me. If I try to defeat my flesh in my own power, it will beat me every time. That is why we have to be careful. Paul told the Romans, "For sin shall not be master over you, for you are not under law, but under grace" (Romans 6:14).

Law and Grace

I was preaching out of the book of 1 John one time, talking about "the world and the lusts thereof are passing away." I was trying to make the point that the older you get, the less you are tempted to sin. I told a story about four old boys who were playing golf. One guy got up to the tee, and a frog jumped up near his pantleg and began to tug on it.

"Hey, buddy!" the frog yelled.

"What?" the man asked, noticing that his friends had also heard the frog.

"If you'll kiss me on the lips, I'll become the most beautiful woman you've ever seen in your life. I'll live with you until the day you die, and you'll never be unsatisfied with me."

The guy looked down at the frog for a long time. All of his friends got very quiet to see what he was going to do. Finally that old guy picked up the frog, unzipped the pocket on his golf bag, placed the frog in it, and zipped it up. One of his friends said, "What are you doing? Didn't you hear what the frog said?"

"Yeah," he replied, "but at my age I'd rather have a talking frog!"

As I got older, I thought my temptation would become easier. But one of my elders, a 75-year-old man I really respect, grabbed my attention after we finished the service that night.

"Wayne!" he yelled at me across the auditorium.

"Yeah, Chuck?"

"Wayne, you missed it!"

"What do you mean?"

"I don't know about you, brother, but if it was me, I'd kiss the frog."

As he walked out the door, it dawned on me what he was saying: *The flesh doesn't get better.* Temptation is going to be temptation, no matter how old we get. Now that I've gotten older, I'd have to say that temptation only worsens. The older you get, the more experience you have, the more the flesh can beset you. That's why Paul told the believers in Rome, "Sin shall not be master over you, for you are not under law, but under grace" (Romans 6:14). Most of us live our lives with sin dominating us. We go day to day battling the same old temptations and making the same old mistakes. But Paul says that sin shall not dominate us because we are not under law.

Law and grace work under two different principles, although the standard does not change: God still demands perfection and purity from us. Under law, it is up to me to attain it. Under grace, He has put His Spirit within me to enable me to attain it. The difference is that while I live under grace, I am enabled to do what God has commanded me to do. So if I am going to church, and I get on the interstate frustrated and upset, it is obvious that the flesh is dominating me. But if I simply give the situation to the Lord and confess the fact that I know my flesh is wicked, then the Holy Spirit overcomes me. I defeat Satan's plan and my flesh. Victory is not me overcoming my flesh; victory is Jesus overcoming me.

My focus has to shift from *law* to *Christ*, who lives in me. Then God can enable me to be what He has commanded me to be. Romans 6 explains what it means to be under grace, but it sounds too easy, and because we are naturally drawn to law, we ignore Scripture's instruction and go right back to finding laws to follow.

A person can be under any kind of law. I remember when I put myself under the "quiet time law." I read a book by a fellow who said, "Everybody who is spiritual gets up at 5:00 in the morning." I thought to myself, "I want to be spiritual," so I got up at 5:00 in the morning. I got on my knees to pray, and made a big mistake: I closed my eyes. At about 6:30 I finally woke up. I wasn't any more spiritual, but I did have sore knees. My mistake was not in wanting to pray, nor in wanting to be spiritual, but in trying to achieve it in the flesh by putting myself under a "quiet time law."

Some people put themselves under a church law. They go to church every Sunday morning, every Sunday night, and Wednesday night, hoping this will make them spiritual. But what happens when they can't get there some Sunday night? I had a guy come to me and complain, "Wayne, I didn't go to church last Sunday, and all day long I was miserable." I said to him, "What are you doing? Is your faith in your church attendance or in the One who lives in you and who is with you all day long? You are putting your faith in the wrong thing."

Being under law is a problem that most people have. Paul wasn't just writing of the Mosaic law, but of all the laws we choose to put over us. We set up rules of behavior, thinking they will make us appear more religious, but they are still nothing but laws. Christian, *we are not under law; we are under grace.* Grace operates under the principle that God lives in us to enable us to do what He has commanded us to do. Grace is not the license to do as you please, but the power to do as you should.

New Person, New Problem

When you are frustrated in living the Christian life, your focus has shifted away from Christ, allowing your flesh to overpower you. But the flesh cannot maintain a satisfactory relationship with God. If it could, Christ would not have had to come and die. We flip-flop back and forth between trying to live a good life and feeling guilty that we can't do it.

I say it's time we stop trying to pretend we can banish sin from our bodies. We are all addicted to sin. Paul said in Romans 7:14 that our flesh is continuously lured toward sin. Whether it is "religious sin," with all its standards, laws, and principles, or outright "rebellious sin," there is still a lure for the flesh. We are all drawn toward it, and there isn't anybody who is immune.

Going to church, reading the Bible, and tithing are all good things, but they can also become external exercises, "laws" that we keep to feel spiritual. By doing so we are just putting ourselves under law again. There is never a time when we cease to be attracted to sin. We can't beat the flesh. *That is why Christ has to overcome us.* He has already defeated Satan; now He wants to overcome us. Christians have to learn the difference of walking after the Spirit and walking after the flesh. The principle of grace is that I am a brand-new person in Christ. I have Someone living in me. Being under grace starts with Christ making me a new creature.

Why did this Life come to live in me? Paul says in Romans 6:6, "Knowing this, that our old self was crucified with Him, that our body of sin might be done away with, that we should no longer be slaves to sin." Even though I still sin, sin no longer has mastery over me. I'm living under a new principle now. If I am under grace, the reality is that sin doesn't have to rule me. There is Someone who lives in me to do through me what I couldn't do by myself.

Paul tells us that sin no longer has to reign in us, for God's Spirit lives inside each one of us. "For he who has died is freed from sin. Now if we have died with Christ, we believe that we shall also live with Him" (Romans 6:7,8). A few verses later he tells us, "Therefore do not let sin reign in your mortal body that you should obey its lusts" (Romans 6:12). In other words, I have a choice that I have to start making. I can learn to start cooperating with the Spirit that lives in me, or I can keep trying to do things on my own. The former will lead to success, the latter to further frustration.

Romans 6:1-5 basically says, "I'm a new person, but I have a new problem." The problem is that although I have the Spirit of God living in me, my flesh hasn't changed. Believers have a major battle going on that a non-Christian can never experience. When I was lost, the flesh just dominated me. The law condemned me because I was under God's holy standard of justice. Now that Christ has met that standard on my behalf, I have been put under grace, but the flesh is still there. So Christ lives in me to overcome it—I just have to learn to cooperate! I have to learn how to say no to the lustful desires of the flesh, and I can do that now in the power that God has given me.

That's why Romans 6:13 tells us, "Do not go on presenting the members of your body to sin as instruments of unrighteousness; but present yourselves to God as those alive from the dead, and your members as instruments of righteousness to God." In other words, I have to learn to make a presentation. Rather than always chasing after sin, I have the power to present myself as an instrument of holiness to the Lord. I have to put my focus on yielding to Christ, not on not yielding to sin. That's why I appreciate the message of Romans 6:13. Whereas the previous verse tells me, "Don't obey your lusts," in verse 13 my focus shifts away from lust and toward the Lord. If I continue to focus on sin, I'm sure to fail. But if I learn to present myself to Christ, I find a new power—His life in me. That's why victory is not me overcoming sin, but Christ overcoming me.

Fixing Our Eyes on Jesus

How many times have you gotten on your knees and said, "O Lord, I had lustful thoughts today. I confess them to You, and I ask You to forgive me of them." Then you get up off your knees and those lustful thoughts come right back to dominate you the rest of the day. What happened? *You focused on the wrong thing.* Once you've confessed your sin, it's time to refocus on something greater. *Fix your eyes on the Lord Jesus,* so that He in His power can overcome you. That is the key to living a new life.

My daddy used to raise bird dogs when I was little, and I loved the cute, frisky puppies best. But the frisky dogs were the ones that caused my father the most trouble. It's natural for dogs to want to chase birds, so my dad had to retrain them to point instead of chase. He had to help them learn how to focus on the hunt, not just the chase. A pup might have all the necessary tools—big feet, long legs, and a great sense of direction—but if he won't learn to point at the birds instead of chasing after them, he's worthless as a bird dog.

I'll never forget the time one of those frisky dogs went tearing out after some birds. He made the mistake of racing right by my dad, who hauled off and slugged that dog upside the head. The dog went flying, rolled down the hill, and staggered to his feet. An amazing thing happened then. He immediately started chasing after those birds, but this time, as he got close, he suddenly froze, pointing directly at them. I'm sure it was a tough way to learn a lesson, but that dog became a great bird dog that day. He learned the importance of focusing on the right thing.

The more I am in the Word, the more I am seeking to be yielded to Christ, the more I am going to be consciously aware of Someone living in me and overcoming me in my areas of sin. But if all I ever do is focus on my fleshly problems, I'm stuck trying to defeat them in my own power.

I was preaching this message in our church a while back, and a lady came forward to say, "I've never heard this before. Can I have a tape of it?"

"Sure," I told her. "Do you want to hear it again?"

"Actually, I want to send it to my husband."

"Where is he?"

"In the penitentiary," she replied.

"What for?"

"Pornography."

She never got any more specific than that, but he was sentenced for 50 years, so it had to have been something pretty bad. As I handed her the tape, she looked at me and said, "My husband has been to every counselor known to man to overcome his problem, but nothing has helped. He can't control it. Nobody has ever had the courage to tell him that he'll never overcome sin himself, but that Christ can overcome him. I think for the first time I have the answer he has been searching for. He says he loves the Lord, but he is stuck in his sin. If he will change his focus from fighting sin to yielding to Christ, and let the Lord enable him, then Christ can overcome him. That's the difference, isn't it?"

I assured her it was, and we knelt to pray for her husband to refocus his life. He'll never beat his addiction to pornography, but Christ in him can.

Dominated by the Flesh

Why can't we beat the flesh? Because our flesh is addicted to sin. Only Christ in us can break that addiction. He can break sin's power over us. It may keep tempting us, but it will no longer have dominion over us. We don't have to be slaves to sin anymore.

The apostle Paul, in writing to a young church with some severe problems, took pains to instruct the believers in the importance of letting Christ live through them. When he wrote to the church in Corinth, he explained to them in 1 Corinthians 1:2-9 what they ought to be like, then he took the rest of the book to skin them alive for their failure to live that way!

What was wrong with them is found in 1 Corinthians 3:1: "And I, brethren, could not speak to you as to spiritual men, but as to men of flesh, as to babes in Christ." Paul pointed back to when he first came to Corinth, when the people had been worshiping idols. In Acts 18, which describes the founding of the church in Corinth, Paul was working as a tentmaker, sharing the gospel with both Jews and Greeks. The people were dead in their sins, and when they met Jesus Christ they became spiritually alive, but they were spiritual babies.

Of course, there's nothing wrong with being a baby, but all babies have to mature. In 1 Corinthians 3:2,3 Paul offers this indictment: "I gave you milk to drink, not solid food; for you were not yet able to receive it. Indeed, even now you are not yet able, for you are still fleshly." The word for "fleshly," is the same word he uses in Romans 7:14 to describe people who were "slaves" to sin. They were dominated by their flesh—saved people living like unsaved.

The problem Paul brings out here is that the believers of Corinth were still yielding to the flesh and chasing after it, rather than putting their focus on Jesus Christ. He says, "For since there is jealousy and strife among you, are you not fleshly, and are you not walking like mere men?" (1 Corinthians 3:3). You see, the Corinthian church had succumbed to the flesh. They had never come out of the nursery. Babies always cling to fleshly things, and these people were nothing but babes in Christ.

I remember when my daughter Stephanie was little. We were in her bedroom together when a thunderstorm was going on, and my daughter kept sticking her head under the blankets. I said, "Stephanie, don't be afraid. Jesus is here."

But Stephanie just looked at me and said, "Daddy, will you tell Him to leave, because He is scaring me to death!"

My little girl wanted *me* to be there, because she could see and touch and feel me, but she wasn't too sure about this invisible God. That's the way children think—concretely. They believe in what they can feel and see. A baby has the attitude of the flesh and the activity of the flesh. But mature adults must move beyond that, and recognize that God is with us, even in the thunderstorms of life.

The Corinthian church is a perfect picture of Christians. Look at all the problems in that church. Paul describes jealousy, strife, and divisions. The Corinthians attached themselves to men instead of attaching themselves to Christ. In chapter 4 he told them they had become arrogant. The word he used was a compound word meaning both "spiritual" and "wind." In other words, these people were spiritual airbags. They bragged about their spiritual lives, but there was nothing to them. For all their talk, the church at Corinth had some pretty serious problems. In chapter 5 Paul mentions incest in the church and their lack of willingness to deal with it. In chapter 6 they were suing one another, refusing to solve their differences. Chapter 7 deals with wrong views concerning marriage, divorce, remarriage, and singleness. When you look at the book of Corinthians, you see a living example of how the flesh can continue to dominate believers. Our flesh is still addicted to sin. So we have to learn a new way of living to overcome that addiction.

The flesh is going to be sinful. We are all addicted to sin. Our bodies are devoted to it. But our flesh can be overcome by the message of grace. We are children of God— the very products of His grace. We are no longer under law, so sin should not have mastery over us. The key to making that important change is for you to realize that you can never completely overcome sin, but Christ can overcome you.

The Rest of Grace

3

Shifting into Neutral

When I was growing up, my dad had an old Studebaker. (If you're in your twenties, you may not know what I'm referring to. I'll date myself by telling you that in the 1950s Studebakers were among America's more popular cars. Since they ceased being made in 1963, you may never have seen one.) By today's design standards, the Studebakers were a bit strange. They were shaped like a bullet, to put it simply. Ours was yellow, and as a kid I thought it was pretty special to have a yellow bullet parked in the driveway.

In those days it was cheaper for my dad to buy bus tokens and ride the bus to work than to drive his Studebaker, so the yellow bullet stayed home while my dad was at work. In the summer of my twelfth year, the urge to fire the bullet overcame me. I decided to learn to drive the car—on my own. I had watched my dad work the clutch and gears hundreds of times, and knew I could do it.

My inaugural run in the Studebaker was a success—all 20 feet of it. I cranked the engine, pushed in the clutch, put the transmission in reverse, and navigated backward the length of the driveway. Carefully I shifted into first gear and returned the bullet to its assigned position in the driveway.

These trips continued daily that summer and beyond—20 feet forward, 20 feet back, 20 feet forward, 20 feet back. Conservatively, I figure that by the time I got my driver's license I had been around the world at least three or four times—20 feet at a time.

During my excursions in the yellow bullet, I learned a lesson that has served me well in my spiritual life. In fact, it's the lesson that's at the heart of the Christ life. I learned that when I shifted the transmission into neutral and pushed down on the accelerator, the engine would roar with pent-up power, but the car wouldn't move an inch. It wouldn't go anywhere.

What was going on? Had the transmission fallen out of the car? Of course not. All the elements for motion were there—engine, fuel, transmission—but as the driver, I had neutralized the connection between the elements. With the transmission in neutral, the yellow bullet's power matched its appearance—pitiful! With the gears in neutral, it wouldn't go forward and it wouldn't go back. It wouldn't do anything. It just made a loud noise. Only when I, as the person in control, shifted it into gear did the power of the car move it where I wanted it to go. It began to dawn on me that *I* was in charge, not the car. The car was my servant, and it was my decision to empower it to move forward, move back, or not move at all.

This is what we must understand about the Christ life. There is a power in my life just waiting to propel me forward onto a dangerous road leading to sin. The Bible calls that power the flesh, or the self. But I am still in the driver's seat, choosing whether or not to engage the gears which release the power. And the reason I now have a choice is because of Christ living in me. When Christ came to live in me, He shifted the power of sin into neutral. The "transmission" didn't fall out—anyone who has struggled with sin knows that. But with sin shifted into neutral, our engine may roar loudly, but it has no power.

The Selfishness of Sin

The reason that's important is because Paul tells us that "our old self was crucified with Christ" (Romans 6:6). What does he mean by the "old self"? When we were born, we were born as descendants of Adam, the first man. Romans 5:12 says, "Therefore, just as through one man sin entered into the world, and death through sin, and so death spread to all men, because all sinned." Because Adam and Eve fell into sin, all who followed them as human beings were born with the virus of Adam's sin. Sin is as much a part of our human nature now as sinlessness was a part of Adam's and Eve's nature before they sinned. The very constitution of humanity was changed when our first parents sinned.

When we talk about sin we are talking about a transgression of that which God requires of us. Sin is missing the mark—the target, so to speak—that God has designed. "Self" is the same thing as the flesh. When I am dealing with the flesh, I'm dealing with the self life instead of the Christ life. That's one of the reasons I call the Christian life the Christ life, because it immediately brings into contrast who is in control—Christ or me. The self life is flesh—me, my, I. In fact, a close look at the word "sin" makes it clear: "I" is at the center of sin. Therefore, the self-life (the life empowered by sin) is based on what *I* want, not what God wants.

It's important to keep our terms straight—self and flesh are identical. Sin is the result of self and flesh, and it misses the mark of what God requires. Sin is selfishness, or self-centeredness instead of God-centeredness. Self says, "I'll do what I want, when I want, how I want." Obviously, unless you live on an island by yourself, this makes living with other people pretty difficult! If I have problems in my marriage, for instance, I can almost always trace either the problem or a lack of spiritual reconciliation back to self-centered choices on my part. More powerful than the engine in my dad's yellow bullet, the flesh is waiting to be released to propel me into sinful behavior and conflict with others (not to mention conflict with God). At the core of almost all my sinful behavior is the flesh. Sin is simply the outward manifestation of self or flesh.

Who among us is not frozen with fear at the mention of the deadly Ebola virus? Identified in 1976 along the Ebola River in Zaire, Africa, this deadly and contagious virus leads to death in nearly 85 percent of its cases. But there is another virus more deadly than the Ebola—one that kills 100 percent of its carriers. That virus is the virus of sin. The first to be infected were our original parents in the Garden of Eden. Following the naming pattern of the Ebola virus, we might call sin the Eden virus.

All of us were yet unborn in the loins of Adam when Adam sinned. That sin virus was passed into the human race. Once you are born into Adam's family, there is no cure for that virus except the fact that Jesus Christ came to die to pay for the penalty of that virus. He took the death that we deserve because of that virus. He took it upon himself. He rose the third day and then later ascended to heaven. When we put our faith in Him, He takes us out of Adam and puts us into Himself.

Presenting Our Bodies to Christ

Colossians says we have been removed from the kingdom of darkness into the kingdom of His dear Son (Colossians 1:13,14). This is a change that occurs when we are "born again" (John 3:3). We become citizens of a new kingdom, the kingdom of Christ. As a brand-new person, we are not what we used to be. When we were in Adam we were devoid of the Spirit of God. Now that Christ has put His life in us, we are believers and His Spirit lives in us. The old man has been crucified with Him and the life we now live is by virtue of the Son of God living in us (Galatians 2:20).

What a marvelous change has taken place in us through Christ! As I said before, because we are in the driver's seat of our lives we have a choice. Born in Adam, the power of sin was engaged with "the pedal to the metal." We had no choice. Life was a process of hanging on for dear life, like me trying to keep a runaway yellow Studebaker from wreaking havoc in my neighborhood if I had gotten on the street with the accelerator stuck! But Christ has put sin in neutral, and we are no longer forced to be taken where it wants us to go. Through the power of the Holy Spirit in us, we can choose to leave sin in neutral.

In light of this great gift of grace, which enables us to choose, Paul says, "I urge you therefore, brethren, by the mercies of God, to present your bodies a living and holy sacrifice, acceptable to God, which is your spiritual service of worship" (Romans 12:1). Why does he say *"present* your *body"*? Because that's our choice—to present ourselves to God rather than to sin. We must daily learn to present our body to Him, so that our body of sin might remain in neutral. Don't get the idea that our flesh, the potential to sin, ceases to exist. We still have our physical flesh and our spiritual flesh. I could talk to anyone reading this book and see that your body has not left you. It's funny, my body just follows me around. When I got saved, I still had the same body I had when I was lost. The same potential to sin is still there, but the power not to sin is there as well. When we present our bodies to God as a living sacrifice, we shift the power of sin into neutral and we engage His power.

The Christian needs to learn this principle. When you live surrendered to Christ, it is the same attitude of dependence that you had at the moment of your salvation. Colossians 2:6 says, "As you therefore have received Christ

Jesus the Lord, so walk in Him." The same desperation you had when you cried out to Him, realizing the futility of living life in your own strength, is the attitude that must permeate your whole Christian life. When you live that way, sin can roar at you but it has no power because it is in neutral. However, when you step outside the realm of His will and surrender to Him, the flesh takes over because it is bound to sin. You will end up crashed on a dead-end street.

Because of the process of growing in maturity in Christ, we are going to sin in this life. But when we do, we should confess it and repent of it. Repentance doesn't simply mean that we say we won't sin again, but that we realize we will now submit and surrender to Christ. We again offer ourselves as a living sacrifice to God, willing to do His will instead of our own. This gives Christ a renewed opportunity to live His life through us, accomplishing what we cannot accomplish on our own.

In the Driver's Seat

The last part of Romans 6:6 says, "We should no longer be slaves to sin." That is the whole message. If I'm submitted to Christ, allowing Him to be my life, then He neutralizes the addiction that my body has to sin. He becomes the antidote to the Eden virus. Then I can live in the victory that He already has given me in Himself. Victory is not something I look forward to; it is something I have. It is the Person of Christ living in me.

Therefore, who is responsible for my sin? I have to realize that *I am*. I am in the driver's seat of my life, and if the power of sin comes alive in me, then it was I who shifted it into gear. I can't blame my brother, my mother, my wife, my children, or my circumstances. If there is sin in my life, now that I'm a believer, *I am* responsible for it. Christ has freed me from the penalty of sin, and He has freed me from the power of sin. If it has any power over me at all, it is because I have shifted it back into gear. I have taken it out of neutral by my own choice.

When we become believers, we start realizing that there is a struggle. If we keep sin in neutral, it means we are yielding to the lordship of Christ. He is in the driver's seat. But because sin is so powerful in our bodies, we sometimes give in to it. This is the heart of spiritual warfare.

Many people think that spiritual warfare is like a constant sword fight with demon spirits. This scenario of spiritual warfare has demons constantly poking at us with their fiery darts. We are resigned to living life like the builders of Nehemiah's wall, with a trowel in one hand and a sword in the other (Nehemiah 4:16-23). Of course, the demons and Satan are out there; let's not help their cause by minimizing their opposition to us and Christ's work in us. But in reality, the biggest enemy that you or I will ever face is the one we look at in the mirror when we wake up in the morning. We are in a war from the time we get saved until the time Jesus comes back—a war with our flesh, our sin nature. Our minds have to constantly be renewed by the Word of God.

Many people have come to me and said, "Boy, Satan really got after me today!" Isn't that actually a bit of an arrogant statement? Since Satan can only be at one place at one time, then evidently you are living such a godly life that he had to give up whatever he was doing somewhere else on earth to come and attack you! You must be really spiritual. If you are that spiritual, then you probably don't need to be reading this book. For me, warfare is me dealing with Wayne Barber every day. Wayne Barber's flesh is the biggest battle I'll ever have.

Do I mean to say that Satan and his demons aren't part of the battle at all? Of course not. He is the one putting temptations in front of me. He is the one working in and through the world system to make godly living less appealing. He is the one whispering to me in moments of decision. But he is not the chooser. I am, and you are. When we sin, it is because we choose to submit to desires other than Christ's.

Learning to Submit to God

Don't forget—the first part of having Satan flee from you is to submit to God. James 4:7 says, "Submit therefore to God. Resist the devil and he will flee from you." Submitting to God, in James' words, is the same thing as Paul's words to present ourselves as a living sacrifice. You have to submit first, and then that submission is your resistance to the satanic powers around you.

When we shift the gear of the flesh out of "neutral" and into "sin," we have to understand that it is our responsibility. A Christian can never blame anybody but himself for sin. We have been delivered from the penalty of sin and the power of sin. Now it becomes a real issue daily as we deal with sin and its consequences.

A man in our church had been married to his wife for years, then it was revealed that he had been unfaithful to her over a long period of time. With heavy hearts our church leaders proceeded with the steps of church discipline outlined in Matthew 18:15-17. First, the person who became aware of the affair went to him, and he responded by defending his actions. "Listen," he said, "you don't know what it's like living with my wife. It's all her fault. I deserve better. I met this woman who was having the same experience with her husband. We got together, and I don't see anything wrong with it."

Next, two men went together and confronted him, and he justified his actions again. The third step in our church discipline is that we send the person a certified letter telling him that we are going to expose his sin and his lack of repentance in the next church meeting if he is not willing to repent.

That fellow got that letter, and it really convicted him. He finally began to realize the consequence of the choice he had made. He went before the Lord, and God broke him. One Sunday night as I was preparing to preach, he appeared at my door. "Wayne," he said, "can I share with the people tonight? There is something on my heart."

"What's on your heart?"

"I want to get up in front of the people and admit to them that my affair is my sin. *I'm* the one that's responsible. Nobody but me. I need to ask the church to forgive me, and I want to ask my wife to forgive me. I've already asked her privately, but I want her to know that it is real in my heart."

In spite of the fact that he was not the type of person to speak in front of a group, he did that night. He was completely broken. The whole church immediately identified with him because we are all responsible for our sin. We sang the hymn "Oh, the Blood of Jesus" while I had the women come and get around his wife and the men gather around him. It was one of the sweetest times we've ever had in our church and it came as a result of a man being willing to take responsibility for his own actions.

Every believer has to do that. There is no other person and no spirit that we can blame. There is no circumstance or situation. Jesus has shifted our flesh into neutral. If our flesh has been shifted into gear, it was *our* hand that was at the controls. And the only way it will be put back into neutral is by our hand as well.

4

Surrendering to God

The term "surrender" has to become part of the vocabulary of the believer. At first this is a difficult concept to grasp, because surrender suggests weakness or defeat. No one likes to think of himself or herself as weak or defeated. Yet it is in surrender that victory in the spiritual life begins. The way I begin to get victory over sin is when I surrender to the One who has rendered it powerless.

In World War II, when Japan surrendered to America, the Japanese emperor came forward to make a formal declaration. Instead of saying, "We surrender; we give up," he pulled out his sword and presented it to General MacArthur, the commander of the victorious Allied forces in the South Pacific. Basically what he was saying was, "I will not fight you anymore. We are giving up our weapons and submitting to you." Were the Japanese weak and defeated? Certainly in one sense they were. On the other hand, they had enough troops and munitions to allow them to continue to wage war for many more days.

But here is what goes through the mind of any reasonable person who comes to the point of surrender: "Yes, I could fight harder and further, but likely to no avail. I will, in strength of character, submit myself to this one who is greater, and trust that a greater good will be the outcome." It would have accomplished nothing for Japan to totally destroy her people and resources by fighting a losing battle.

To me the idea of surrender is when you come before God and you say, "God, I'm not going to fight You. I'm not going to resist You anymore. I recognize that You are greater than I am, and that it is in my present and eternal best interests to allow You Your rightful place in my life." We only have peace with God through our Lord Jesus Christ. That peace is effected in our lives through surrender, just as it was in the South Pacific when the Japanese emperor gave up his sword, the symbol of his country's power.

Laying Down Our Swords

What is the sword that we as believers hand over to God when we surrender to Him? It is nothing more than our will. When we give up our will to God, we take our hand off the controls and disengage the power of sin in our lives. Like my dad's old Studebaker, the engine can be roaring, but without being in gear it is going nowhere. I remain safe and secure in the driveway, out of trouble, unless I put it in gear.

When we lay down our will before Him, we say, "God, I'm not going to fight You anymore. Here is my will. Please accept it as the symbol of all the strength which in times past I have brought to bear upon the issues of my life—and at times in opposition to You. I am giving up my will and strength in order to gain Yours." It is at that moment, and repeated moments like it throughout our lives, that we begin to gain strength. It is Christ giving us His strength now that our strength has been surrendered.

Let's be even more clear at this point: Don't confuse surrender with commitment. There is a place for commitment in the Christian life, but this is not it. God is not asking us to become more committed—committed to trying harder, sinning less, and being better. I am talking about *surrender,* not commitment. Surrender is when we *stop trying to win* instead of being committed to trying harder.

Here's another word to use for surrender: *yield.* What do you do when you come to a "Yield" sign while driving your car? You usually come to a stop to let another car pass, don't you? Then what is the difference between a "Stop" sign and a "Yield" sign? The difference is found in the element of the other car. If another car is approaching, you are obligated to give way to it, which usually requires stopping. Without the presence of the other car, you can go on ahead without stopping. So a "Yield" sign says, "You are required to surrender *your* desire to the desire of the approaching car. You must surrender to the other person."

Trust me on this one: At the intersections of your spiritual life, God is always approaching in the other car. Always. That means that you are always going to be required to yield. And if you don't? Well, you have my sympathies. You are headed for a horrendous crash with the living God, because He is not going to yield to the likes of you and me. He has the right of way in the heavens and on the earth. And the sooner we learn it, the sooner we will stop colliding with, and instead begin cooperating with, the good things that God wants to accomplish through our lives.

Yielding, or surrendering, to God is a 24-hour-a-day, moment-by-moment attitude. It is an attitude before it is ever an activity. It is a willingness not to fight God, but to let Him be who He wants to be in my life. If that attitude prevails, we will begin to enter into the victory that we already have. Hear me again: *Victory is not something we work toward; it is something we live from.* In other words, victory is not something we are seeking; it is something that has been won. Christ is our victory. He is the One who rendered sin powerless.

We surrender to Him because it is in Him that victory is enjoyed. Christ rendered sin powerless by what He did on the cross. He paid the penalty. He rendered sin powerless in our lives by conquering it, defeating it, and paying its penalty. By His Holy Spirit, He lives His life in us, which now conquers the power of sin. Christ, our Victor over sin, lives in us! Even though the flesh is still lured to sin and addicted to it, Christ living in us has power over it. We have to learn to surrender to the only One who has power over sin, so that we might therefore have power over sin as well.

The whole key to understanding the concept of surrender is found in Ephesians 3:14-21 in the prayer that Paul prays. The whole book of Ephesians hinges on this one prayer. It sums up everything in chapters 1, 2, and 3, and sets up everything in chapters 4, 5, and 6. Ephesians 3:16,17 has the answer to how I practically go about surrendering to Christ day by day. The apostle Paul begins by saying, "That He would grant you, according to the riches of His glory, to be strengthened with power through His Spirit in the inner man." The word "strengthened" means "given ability that you don't have." The phrase "according to" sets the standard for how we are strengthened. We are strengthened according to the riches of God's glory.

If I were a rich man and wanted to give you a gift, would you want me to give it to you "out of" my wealth or "according to" my wealth? Let's say I have a million dollars, and "out of" my wealth I give you a gift that cost me a dollar. You would be grateful, but perhaps a bit confused, for a dollar gift certainly doesn't reflect my ability as a gift giver. Anyone with a million dollars can afford to give gifts worth far more than a dollar. But if I give you a gift "according to" my wealth, my gift would reflect the wealth that is mine.

Therefore, when Paul prays for the Ephesians to be strengthened "according to the riches of Christ's glory," that is not some token phrase. It is not "out of," for like the dollar gift, we might be strengthened just a little bit. No, His strengthening is "according to," consistent with, His infinite riches. How much strengthening would you expect to receive from One who has infinite strength? Enough so you can really live in the victory that Christ has offered to you through Himself when you are willing to be surrendered to Him and strengthened by Him.

Paul tells the Ephesians, "To me, the very least of all saints, this grace was given, to preach to the Gentiles the unfathomable riches of Christ" (Ephesians 3:8). The riches of Christ are unfathomable and unsearchable. His riches are like a well that has no bottom. For all eternity, the riches of His glory will never be exhausted. He also tells the Ephesians that the only way they will understand it is for their eyes to be opened. He says, "I pray that the eyes of your heart may be enlightened, so that you may know what is the hope of His calling, what are the riches of the glory of His inheritance in the saints" (Ephesians 1:18).

Ephesians 1:3 describes what I like to call the First National Bank of God. Paul says, "Blessed be the God and Father of our Lord Jesus Christ, who has blessed us with every spiritual blessing in the heavenly places in Christ." Now anything that has to do with spiritual blessing is already ours in Christ Jesus. People ask me occasionally, "Wayne, do you have the second blessing?" I'm thinking, "Hey, I've got the millionth blessing because I've got the One who has already blessed me with every spiritual blessing."

A Road Map of Blessings

I was preaching at a church in West Texas when a lady I did not know came to me at the end of one of the services. This was a leading church in that area which taught a great deal about the "sign" gifts of the Spirit. All week I had preached, "You don't need anything but Jesus, and you already have Him. Your experiences will be experiences that will result in surrender to Him." The lady chased me down in the parking lot the last day of the conference and through her tears said, "Wayne, all my life I've been seeking the gifts, but finally it's dawned on me that I already have the Giver of the gifts." That's the truth. Be strengthened according to the riches of Christ Jesus. Every spiritual blessing is already resident in Him, and He lives in you.

You can walk through Ephesians verse by verse and be blessed by reading about your blessings. Let's follow Paul's road map of blessings:

- In Ephesians 1:1 he says that we are saints. While the world thinks of Mother Teresa when saints are discussed, God thinks of you and me! He has put us into the category of "holy ones" because we are found in the Holy One, Jesus Christ.

- In Ephesians 1:4 he says in effect, "He has chosen us; He hasn't rejected us." The height of being accepted is being chosen. The most stressful part of the day for many schoolchildren is whether they are chosen first or last at recess when ball teams are being formed. But Christians can relax on this issue, since they have already been chosen for permanent membership on God's first-string team. While some people go through life without any sense of identity, believers are identified with Christ. We have been chosen by Him.

- In Ephesians 1:5 Paul tells us that we have been adopted as sons. We are adopted as children of God, and that adoption process goes on until the day we receive a glorified body to dwell in for eternity. In the Roman law, nobody could reject an adopted child. We as believers are forever secure in Christ. We cannot lose our salvation. Romans 8:23 says we are looking forward to the completion of our adoption one day when we will receive a glorified body.

- Ephesians 1:7 says, "In Him we have redemption through His blood, the forgiveness of our sins." Do you realize that the word "redemption" means we've been purchased off the slave block of sin? We don't have to live enslaved to sin anymore. As hard as it is to imagine in our modern world, Christian believers in some foreign lands are even today being sold into slavery. Some Christian organizations are raising funds to purchase these believers—especially the children—and return them to their freedom. That is what God has done for us. He has redeemed us from the marketplace of sin in order that we might be free.

My son came to me one night and he said, "Dad, I'm having this problem in my thought life. It's really bothering me. I confess it over and over, but it keeps coming back."

"I know what it is."

"Oh no, you don't know what it is."

"Yes, I do, too."

"All right, tell me what it is."

I told him and his mouth dropped open.

"How did you know?"

"You got it from me. I got it from Adam. All of us are tempted, but the key is that you've been redeemed from its power, from its penalty. You are Christ's. You have been bought with a price. If you can understand this, you will not have to yield to that temptation anymore."

Strengthened on the Inside

Paul's prayer in Ephesians 3:16 says, "...that He would grant you...to be strengthened with power." Paul is praying that the Ephesian believers might be strengthened with might through God's Spirit in the inner man. The word "strengthened" means "to be given an ability that you don't naturally have." It is something that God gives to you. You can have dominion over sin through the ability He gives to you by His Spirit in the inner man.

It is interesting that Paul uses the words, "inner man." This is consistent with other places in Scripture which tell us that God is much more interested in the state of our internal life than in our external life (see 1 Samuel 16:7; 1 Peter 3:3,4; Mark 7:14-23). We live in a world where the tendency is to focus on the outer man. I went to a fitness center once, and it was so interesting to see the guys flexing their muscles in the dressing room. They looked in the mirror and as they combed their hair they looked at their muscles rippling up their back. I thought, "I'll never be as strong as these men are." But thankfully, that is not the key to a victorious life. The key is that we are strengthened in our inner man even though the outer man is decaying.

I co-teach on occasion with Kay Arthur, the founder of Precept Ministries. While conducting a teaching ministry in Romania, we discovered that the Christian women don't wear makeup. Kay decided to forgo makeup as well in order not to hinder her message and ministry to the women. I've seen Kay with makeup, and I've seen Kay without makeup, and I want you to know it's much better to see Kay with makeup. Kay came over to me on our first day there and said, "Wayne, please tell me you recognize me." I replied, "You don't look a day over 110 years old." Two weeks later, when we were back home at our church, I saw Kay and said, "Oh, Kay, you look so good." I stopped the service and said, "You know, ladies, some of you think wearing makeup is a sin. I think it's a sin not to wear it. Go cover it up!"

Well, fortunately Kay is a good friend and we can joke together about the negative side of the aging process. But the truth is that the outer man is decaying. Yet while the outer man is decaying, the inner man is growing strong. And the inner man is what God is strengthening.

What is the inner man? Look at verse 17 of Ephesians 3. The inner man is associated with the heart. It is the control center of a person's life. It is where everything comes from: "That Christ may dwell in your hearts through faith." When you first read that verse it looks like it says "in order that," but that is not the word used there. In fact, in the Greek it should be "Christ dwelling in your hearts by faith." The word "dwell" means "to be made to be at home." Have you ever been at somebody's house who made you feel at home? Someone who actually did everything he or she could to accommodate your presence? That's the word used here. Christ has been indwelling you from the moment you were saved. We are now talking about Him being made to be at home in your life as a believer.

Every time I go to the home of my good friends who live in Mississippi, they "make me to be at home." In all humility, I can honestly say that they love me, and they want me to be confident in my knowledge of their love. Because of their love for me, their home is my home. I am not treated special, but am treated as one of their family— which has both good points and bad points!

For instance, they keep two sticks by the basketball goal in their driveway. When I arrive, it's my job to grab the sticks and fend off their mean watchdog who always confronts any visitor. I get one stick and whoever is with me gets the other stick, and we keep the dog at bay while we get to the house. I know, you're probably thinking, "Gee, if they really loved you they'd lock the dog up." Well, the flip side of the dog story is that I enjoy the dog's protection and watchfulness at night while I'm asleep. My friend's attitude is, "We'll put the sticks out for you. After that, it's up to you just like it's up to us. You're family."

We get inside the house, and there's cake and iced tea sitting on the cabinet for me. There are bedrooms everywhere. They say, "Help yourself. Take whatever bedroom you want to take." I've slept in about every room in that house. That is what it means to be made to be at home in somebody's house. Everything that is needed is provided—from sticks to ward off the watchdog, to food and a place to rest, to access to personal living areas. That's what it's like to be made to be at home, and that's the word Paul uses here.

Obedience and Faith

Why does Paul say we must be strengthened? *"That Christ may dwell in your hearts through faith."* When the word "heart" is used figuratively it means the center of something, like when Jesus spoke of the "heart of the earth" (Matthew 12:40). The heart is that which everything revolves around. The heart of the inner man has to do with the spiritual part of man that is the motivating, controlling area of his life. If you take the word "heart" and follow it through the New Testament, you can put it in many categories. Let's look at three examples.

1. Luke 9:47 says, "But Jesus, knowing what they were thinking in their heart . . ." You may think this is mistranslated and should be "mind" because we don't think with our heart. What does the heart have to do with the mind? Well, Hebrews 4:12 says, "For the Word of God is

living and active and sharper than any two-edged sword, and piercing as far as the division of soul and spirit, of both joints and marrow, and able to judge the thoughts and intentions of the heart." If that heart is surrendered to Christ, then its thoughts are not going to lead the mind astray.

2. Matthew 18:35 says, "So shall My heavenly Father also do to you, if each of you does not forgive his brother from your heart." There are a lot of people in churches who won't surrender their attitudes to Christ. They won't accommodate His presence in those areas of their lives. Our attitudes spring from the heart.

3. John 14:1 talks about our emotions: "Let not your heart be troubled; believe in God, believe also in Me." There are many areas of your heart that go deeper than what people can see. If you've offered Him the sword of your will, if you're not willing to fight Him anymore but are willing to let Him have control, that's what surrender is all about.

How do you actually accommodate Him in those areas? Through faith. The word "faith" can also be translated "believe." You cannot separate obedience and faith. They are like two sides of a coin. You can tell people about your faith, but that shows them nothing. The way you obey God tells them everything about what you really believe.

If I'm willing to obey Christ I will let His Word get into my mind. It is when I obey His Word that I am surrendering. That is my act of surrender—giving up doing my will and doing His will instead. That is what it means to accommodate Him in the different areas of my heart.

If there is an area of your life that you have not yet surrendered to Christ and to what His Word says, it is obvious that you are not realizing the victory that He has won for you in that area of your life. But as you learn to surrender to Him and His Word, then you begin to walk in the realization of what He means by rendering sin power-less. We have to develop the attitude of surrender. We are enabled by His grace so that we can be strengthened according to the riches in His glory in the inner man.

For example, if I am struggling with immorality, I must go to the Word and find out what God says about immorality. The Word is very clear: "Flee immorality" (1 Corinthians 6:18). You then begin to understand that God already has a design in His Word; He has already spoken. If we take the Word and let it reign supreme in our hearts, doing what God says to do in His power, than we realize His victory.

Sometimes obeying God may seem unreasonable. Would it seem unreasonable to get rid of a television set if immorality is a problem for you? Perhaps. But God's Spirit may convict you to do that when you see how serious sin is and what a hold it has on your life. But awaiting the outcome of that "unreasonable" decision is the blessing of the victory that He promised if you would obey Him.

How do you surrender? Wherever the flesh is attempting to gain control, allow the Spirit to show you how to obey the Word. For instance, if you sense as you are studying the Scriptures that God is revealing an area of sin to you, don't resist Him. Surrender to the Spirit of God! Offer up your will to Him. When He moves upon your heart, do whatever He tells you to do without delay.

Obedience—the act of yielding to God so as to avoid a collision with Him—is the act of surrender which allows Christ's victory to be found in your life.

What Is God Doing to Me?

Once when I was leading a youth retreat, we had a lot of chairs to move to another building. Seeing one of our key youth leaders sitting under a nearby tree, I called, "Hey, Chris, I really need your help." Chris replied, "No, I just need to sit under the tree a little while and meditate and think about what the Lord wants me to do right now."

I wanted to give him a good swift kick in the backside and get him over there where we needed his help. Was it possible that the Lord was really speaking to Chris at that moment, telling him to stay put? Of course—and it was not my place to judge. But here's my point: There is some confusion among Christians when they equate passivity with spirituality. That is, they think it is more spiritual to "wait upon God" than to put their hand to the plow (Luke 9:62). That is the danger of spiritual passivity.

When you think about the life God wants to live through you, it is dangerous to develop this idea of passivity. "Well, I'll just sit under a tree and let God do everything. God will get the chairs moved. God will help my neighbor. God will overcome this sin in my life." People fall into the trap of thinking that the spiritual life is all God and none of us. But if you look closely at the commands in

Scripture, you find that there are many things that we alone are responsible to do.

Actually, the Christian life is what I like to call a 200 percent relationship. One hundred percent is God's power and presence at work in me, and the other hundred percent is my willingness to cooperate with Him in obedience. God has a part and I have a part. His part is to provide power and victory for living. My part is the choice I make to obey Him so that He can do His part. As noted earlier, Romans 12:1,2 shows us what we are responsible to present ourselves as a living sacrifice to God. The "living" part shows that we remain alive after becoming a sacrifice. The "sacrifice" part means that we are dead to ourselves, which is how we become alive to God. You just can't leave this piece of the puzzle out. Yes, it is God working through us, but it is also *us* willing to cooperate with Him in obedience.

Becoming a Living Sacrifice

Romans 12:1 says, "I urge you therefore, brethren, by the mercies of God, to present your bodies a living and holy sacrifice, acceptable to God, which is your spiritual service of worship." A little grammatical insight will help us better understand Paul's command. When he says "present your bodies," the word "present" is in the form of a command. Therefore it is translated "present"—an imperative instruction for Christians.

But there is more. It is also a punctiliar action, meaning a simple, completed event at a point in time rather than a continuing event. When used in a command form, the punctiliar sense says, "Do it. Do it. Do it." The choice is an event, a decision—not a process. And it is a choice we make repeatedly, as often as needed, for the duration of our lives. Contrast this with the choice to receive Christ as one's Lord and Savior. This is a choice made once and for all. However, the decision to present oneself to Christ as a living sacrifice is a decision made countless times through the course of the Christian life.

True, every time we present ourselves to Christ for His will to be done in a difficult area of our life, we wish it would be the last time we have to face that decision. But the reality of life this side of heaven is that temptation conquered *once* is not temptation conquered for all time. We must continue to present ourselves moment by moment, day after day.

By the way, in case you think this sacrifice is an unreasonable command, read on: "This is holy and acceptable to God, which is your [reasonable] spiritual service of worship." The King James and New King James versions say "your reasonable service," while some other translations say "your spiritual service" Whether translated "reasonable" or "spiritual," the key issue is the Greek word *logikos*. Do you see our word "logic" in *logikos*? This word literally meant "rational" in Greek and became "logical" in English. Paul is saying, "In light of the mercies of God, it only makes sense that you present yourself to Him sacrificially. What I am telling you is not unreasonable." It may seem unreasonable beforehand, but once you present yourself to Him, it becomes your reasonable service. It is the only thing that makes sense. The offering that God is looking for is our surrender to Him.

In Romans 12:2 he shows us how to surrender to Him: "And do not be conformed to this world, but be transformed by the renewing of your mind, that you may prove what the will of God is, that which is good and acceptable and perfect." In verse 1 there is a presentation, and in verse 2 there is a transformation and a reformation. The sense given in the J.B. Philips' translation of the New Testament seems best: "Don't let the world around you squeeze you into its own mold." Don't think like they think. Don't act like they act. We are to be pressed into the mold of Scripture. The renewing of our mind is something we can do. That is the renovation, which is our responsibility. The transforming part is what God does. We present, He transforms. If we renovate our mind and present our body to Him, which is rehearsing what Romans 6:12,13 talk about, we will prove what is the "good, acceptable and perfect will of God."

The word "transformed" is from the Greek word for metamorphosis. A metamorphosis in nature is something that happens gradually. It is a natural process, not an unnatural one. It is something to be expected. We are not surprised that a caterpillar becomes a butterfly, or that a tadpole becomes a frog. We have become convinced that this is exactly the way God designed the processes to take place. And it should be the same in the spiritual life, except that our transformation is a *supernatural*, not a natural, transformation.

It is a metamorphosis in the sense that it is a change that is to be expected. When we present ourselves as living sacrifices to God, and when we refuse to be conformed to the world, we will be transformed by the renewing of our mind. "Be transformed" is a marvelous concept. It is an imperative command, but it is in the passive voice, meaning it is done *to* us, not *by* us. In a sense it says, "Submit to the transformation which comes by the renewing of your mind!"

And note that the transformation begins in the mind, not the body. It is something that doesn't change just on the outside, but it changes from the inside out. We have to realize that this is what the grace of God is all about—His transforming power. He does change the externals of our lives, but the externals are only a manifestation of the internals. Eventually other people see it on the outside. An unloving person meets Christ and becomes loving and you think, "What in the world happened?" When your mind is renewed, then the Holy Spirit can transform you from the inside out.

Yielding the Right of Way to God

Are you beginning to get a better picture of what Christianity is all about? It is not an outside changing of anything. People in the world can stop smoking and drinking. They can lose weight and get in shape. But what we are talking about is the change of the *inner man*. A human being cannot reach inside himself and change the "kindness" part of his heart, or the "loving" part of his heart, or the "generosity" part of his heart. That is something God alone can do. When we choose to be loving by surrendering to Him, then the inner transformation can begin, which ultimately will be seen on the outside.

Remember from our previous discussion what happens when we surrender: We simply yield the right of way to God. What appears to be a transformation in us is in reality a greater manifestation of the life of Christ in us. A prideful person becomes humble. A bitter person becomes sweet and gracious. It is Christ on the inside beginning to manifest Himself on the outside through our life. That is the Christ life. But the responsibility we have is that surrender, that dying to self, that willingness to let Him be who He is in us. To do this, we have to realize that we are not by nature loving, joyful, peaceful, patient, kind, good, gentle, faithful, and self-controlled—the fruit of the Holy Spirit from Galatians 5:22,23. But Christ is. The fruit of His life in us is the fruit of His Spirit, the characteristics that others see outwardly. But they begin in the inner man.

I have to come to the place in my life where I am willing to make a presentation of myself to God, and I have to be willing to let his Word renew my mind, so that my life can be totally transformed by the power of His Spirit. That is the 200 percent relationship. He takes care of the transforming. I take care of the renewing, the presenting, and surrendering. I get to tap into the good and acceptable will of God. Anything less than what God says in His Word is less than good, less than acceptable, and less than perfect. I will only know these things to the degree that I am willing to surrender to what God tells me to do. This is the area that I have to work in.

Let me share an illustration of how God taught me this truth. Years ago I had a real problem with bass fishing. By that I don't mean I didn't know how to catch bass. In fact, just the opposite. I knew too well! While there is nothing wrong with bass fishing, it had become an obsession with me. It was dominating my time, my talent, and my treasure. I would tell my wife I was going bass fishing in order to be able to witness to someone. (That was a lie. All I did was invite the person because I wanted to go fishing.) I would go three to five times a week—I have actually cleaned fish with my suit on before I went to church.

One day while I was studying Romans 12:1, God began to convict me that bass fishing had become too much of a priority in my life. The passage says, "Present your bodies a living sacrifice." With that verse God began to show me that I had a problem. It was the strongest leading I've ever had from the Lord on a personal issue in my life. God did not speak to me in audible words, but the Word itself was convicting my mind in a reasonable way. When you are willing to surrender it becomes reasonable and you can sense what God is saying. God put it in my heart that I needed to give up all my fishing equipment.

While we were at a youth camp on a beautiful lake where the fish were biting, the Lord spoke clearly again: "Give up the bass fishing." I replied, "Get behind me, Satan." But of course, that reply was completely of my flesh. The flesh never likes to hear the words "give up" or "yield," or "surrender," or "submit." That's one of the ways you know God has spoken. If it makes your flesh feel better, look out—it may not be God.

Finally I said, "Lord, who do I give my equipment to?"

"Give it to Robert Fortenberry." Robert was a dear friend of mine who is now a missionary in Africa.

"Lord," I argued, "he's already got fishing stuff. As a matter of fact, he's got more stuff than I have. He's even got a boat. I don't have a boat. So I tell You what, Lord. I'll take it all home and sell it. I could use the money."

But I sensed the Lord saying, "No, give it to Robert."

"Lord, I could put it in the closet and not use it for six months."

"Then we would have to deal with it six months later. We need to deal with it now."

Finally I got up in front of the group that night at the camp. I had been through a real time of conviction. God had really worked in that meeting, especially in me. I told everyone to go out and get under a tree and pray for awhile because I wasn't ready to deal with my bass fishing. I felt that if I waited 15 minutes the conviction would go away. Well, the people all went out, but guess who walked in the back door? Robert Fortenberry. He walked straight up to me. I felt like I had seen a ghost. He said, "Wayne, I went outside to pray like you said, and it seemed like God wanted me to come in here and talk to you."

"Well, Robert, is there anything I can help you with?" I said piously, hearing the Lord laughing at me.

"There is nothing I have to say. I feel kind of stupid. Is there anything you want to say to me?"

I sighed and said, "Robert, don't say anything. Just come with me. God wants me to give you something."

I gave him my tackle box with five shelves on both sides. I gave him all the lures in it. I gave him my two fishing rods. I gave him my best reels. I gave him my worm box. I had every kind of worm size, shape, and form. I was proud of that worm box (can you imagine being proud of a box of worms?). Jigs, weights, leaders—I gave it all to him. He looked at me like my elevator had not touched the top floor.

Finally he asked, "Wayne, what's wrong with you?"

"Look, God told me to do it, Robert, so I've done it."

You know, a lot of people will get up and sing these songs that say, "I'll take sickness instead of health, poverty instead of wealth." Just so you know my heart straight out—that's not me. When God calls me to the cross, I go kicking and screaming every time. But when I get there, I find that it is the very place I needed to be all along. I finally did what God had told me to do.

I went home and my wife watched me like I had a viral disease for about three weeks. She could not understand the changes she was seeing. I began to get up early in the morning and have time with God. My whole life began to change. But it wasn't just me who was changing.

She called me one day and said, "Would you come home?"

She was really crying on the phone, and I could only imagine the worst. I thought something was wrong with the children. When I got home she said, "I need to ask you to forgive me." She was broken.

"For what?"

"I've been bitter toward you for the last 4½ years of our marriage—ever since Stephanie was born."

"Bitter?" I was shocked. I always thought I had been the ideal husband.

"Wayne, when Stephanie was born I needed you. You stayed for awhile, but then you took off to West Texas and went deer hunting, leaving me with your mother. I love your mother, but I needed you. You've always done that in my life. I've got to get the poison out of me now. Will you forgive me for holding this against you?"

Remember, hinged to the unreasonable is the unexpected. When you surrender and do what God tells you to do, and as the Spirit opens the eyes of your understanding to apply the Word, you are going to find a blessing on the other side that you didn't even expect.

My wife's confession began a new level of friendship that has grown deeper every year since. We have now been married over 28 years and our relationship is more solid now than it ever has been. Is it a coincidence that my wife's heart was changed on the heels of my own repentance before God? I think not. But remember: We don't repent in order to get an unexpected blessing from God. We repent—surrender, yield, present ourselves as a living sacrifice—because it is the reasonable and worshipful thing to do in light of the mercies of God.

You need to understand that when God takes something away, it is not to hurt you but to help you. God knows what's best in our life. He took the bass fishing away for three years, and then gave it back. This makes it obvious that the point to begin with was not the external thing—bass fishing. It was yielding my heart to God.

God Is Not Out to Get You

Three years after God dealt with my heart about the fishing, my son began to ask me, "Daddy, can we go fishing?" He was about four years old. I thought, "Well, let's pray about it." So my wife and I began to pray about it because we knew that bass fishing could become a habitual pattern in my life again.

The following week a man I had never met before called me from Frankfurt, Kentucky. He said, "I heard your testimony about your bass fishing, and I want you to come over to my house."

I went over to his house and he said, "God has put this burden on my heart, and I have to do it." Then he waved at me and said, "Come into my garage."

I walked into his garage, and it was like walking into a sporting goods store. It was wonderful. He had hand-tied rods and the pistol grips which were popular back then, and he had all the good reels and lures. He handed me a sack full of lures. He gave me a rod and a reel. If I could have, I would have reached up and hugged the Lord. It dawned on me that God never was out to get me. He already *had* me. He was out to help me put things in perspective and choose better priorities in my life.

So my son and I started fishing together. But instead of becoming an addiction, the fishing became a time to bond with my son. It was not used as an escape to get away from my problems. Over the years I have been given all kinds of fishing equipment. As a matter of fact, three years ago someone gave me a brand-new bass boat. I haven't been able to use it more than a dozen or so times, but when I use it, I really enjoy it. It's funny how God has blessed me with that boat, but it is nothing that runs my life anymore. He put my priorities back in perspective. My son and I have had glorious times fishing together.

It is not as if fishing, or any other enjoyable area of life, is wrong. But if you are out of balance, God may take you to a place of imbalance on the other side of the issue to make sure you see things clearly. If you do what He says with no question, you have to be willing to surrender everything to Him. Don't fight Him. Let the Holy Spirit rule. He knows what is good, acceptable, and perfect for your life. He may take you from one extreme to the other extreme, but eventually He brings you to a point of balance.

Victory Through Submission

You may be thinking that bass fishing is not a problem that relates to you. Maybe your problem is swearing. You get up in the morning, read your Bible, and spend time in prayer, but as soon as someone cuts you off on the freeway as you're driving to work, the swearing begins. How do you surrender a wrong attitude of the heart?

The Word is where I go to get answers. If swearing is your weakness, renew your mind with the Word. The mouth is always a revealer of the thoughts of the heart. If a person is willing to deal with that problem God's way, He will renew his mind with the Word. As the mind is renewed with the Word of God, then what is going to come out of the mouth is what is in the mind. So you don't start with the swearing, you start with where it comes from—the heart. You renew the mind with God's Word. The Bible is the key to renewal. If you surrender and obey Him, the Word will automatically take priority in your heart. Jesus said, "If anyone loves Me, he will keep My word"(John 14:23). Christ and the Word go together—you can't separate them.

Some people wrestle with lying. If a person is having trouble telling the truth, he has to come to the Truth, who is Christ. He has to put Christ in his life. There is no deceit that can come out of the mouth of Christ. There is no deceit that will come out of us if Christ is ruling in our life. As a matter of fact, in Ephesians 4 Paul talks about the garment of a Christian when he says "put on the new self" (Ephesians 4:24). He shows that the real garment of a Christian is personal character. He says, "Speak truth, each one of you" (Ephesians 4:25). A person cannot lie when the Holy Spirit is in control of His life. But if self is in control, a person can lie in an instant.

I remember when I first responded to a gospel invitation. I was nine years old, and I wanted to be saved. The preacher said, "Have you ever lied to your mother?" I was thinking to myself, "How do you think I lived to be nine years old? Good grief!" The flesh will lie. Jeremiah 17:9 reads, "The heart is more deceitful than all else." It is a deceiver and a manipulator. Therefore, if I have the right garment on, and my heart is surrendered to Christ, I cannot lie.

Many men deal with an immoral thought life. Again the solution goes back to the Bible. If I renew my mind with the Word of God, the mind will be taken over by the Word. As I surrender to the Word, I step back into the dimension of the One who conquered sin for me. He becomes my victory in that area.

How do I surrender to Him? I give up my sword. I say, "I'm not going to fight You. I'm going to yield and do what You tell me to do." When Japan surrendered to the Allied forces in the South Pacific, they yielded to the presence and authority of those forces. By yielding, they could then have peace. But if Japan ever picked up the sword again, there would be imminent conflict. The conflict is always there when I pick up the sword and start fighting God and His will for me. When I get the attitude "God, don't call me; I'll call you," at that moment I'm defeated. Every weakness of my flesh becomes magnified. When I drop the sword and say, "God, I'm wrong; I surrender," then I once again begin to enjoy the victory that Christ secured at Calvary. Victory is in Him. It is not something He *gives me*; it is something *He is.* So when it is no longer me, that means I'm yielding. It's Him, and He's the victory.

The Exchanged Life

Some preachers, in emphasizing the grace of God, have promoted the term "the exchanged life." The exchanged life concept has ended up confusing people.

Whereas some people tend to live under the law and create new laws (such as the quiet time law, the tithe law, or the church attendance law), the message from some of the exchanged life people has been just the opposite: You don't have to do anything. As a matter of fact, you don't have to confess your sin. It has all been done for you; therefore you don't have any other responsibility. But some people have logically asked, "Wait a minute. If I don't have to do anything, why bother being a Christian?" There can be a lack of balance in the exchanged life message.

This teaching is what really got my attention years and years ago, but it has come to mean different things to different people. If I exchange my life with Christ's life, the exchange takes place when I'm willing to make the choice to surrender. It is no longer me, but Christ living in and through me. As Christ said, no one can serve two masters (Matthew 6:24). No one can serve Christ and himself. There has to be a choice on my part to surrender to him.

In 2 Timothy 2:15 Paul says, "Be diligent to present yourself approved." The word "diligent" carries with it the idea of urgency and an effort to apply yourself. There are many imperatives (commands) in the Christian life, but if we think that because Christ wants to live His life in us, we have exchanged our responsibility for His, we miss the point. Christ says, "Take My yoke upon you" (Matthew 11:29). The yoke is for *two* oxen. The one who is older and more mature is the one who leads the other. When that younger one starts pulling away, the yoke will rub and leave big scars on his neck. He will never get to go where he wants to go because the older one is trained and disciplined to go in the direction it's supposed to go. The whole idea of a yoke is of a cooperative effort. It is one party surrendering to the other. Christ said, "Learn of Me. My yoke is easy. My burden is light." We walk *with* Him in the yoke. Yes, Christ is going to do the leading and the empowering, but I have to learn to make the choice to surrender to Him daily. That will involve getting to know Him, as in any other relationship.

When I first married my wife, I thought I knew her. But I didn't know her like I know her now, 28 years later. We have had to work a lot on developing our relationship with each other. It is the same with a relationship with God. Spending time alone with God and getting into the Word yourself and studying day by day will help you to get to know Him. You don't do works to be spiritual, but to better the relationship you have with Christ. You are developing a love relationship. Your quiet time or devotional hour is not going to make you spiritual—Christ alone is your spirituality. What you are doing is *renewing your mind.* It's going to take time and effort to allow Him to show you how to yield your mind to Him. When you choose to submit to Him, then you will see Him transforming your character.

A Christian coming out of a legalistic background will ask the question, "What do I need to do? What work do I do?" I personally would rather work with somebody coming from the law side, because he already has a sense that he has a responsibility. The greatest preacher of grace in the New Testament was Paul. He came from a background in the law, and saw the responsibility man has under the law.

If you come in totally on the grace side, sometimes you miss the responsibility that man has. You miss the seriousness of sin and the holiness of God. Coming in from the law side, you understand all that. The problem is that you can't perform the way the law demands.

But when you come to understand grace, you realize that nothing has changed as far as what God demands. What has changed is who is qualified to meet those demands, and you discover it is Christ and Him alone.

Our responsibility is not to be perfect, not to win the victory, not to fulfill the law, but *to yield to Christ*, for He alone is our perfection, our victory, and our fulfillment of the law. He now lives in us to enable us to do these things.

So when a person today asks what he should do, the answer is the same one Jesus gave in John 6:29: "This is the work [singular] of God, that you believe in Him whom He has sent." Learn to submit and surrender to Him and to His Word. The rest begins to take care of itself as you know Him better and your mind becomes more sensitive to what His Word says.

It's amazing what happens when you begin to understand these truths. It's like a spiritual fog lifts off your understanding. You start seeing things differently than you saw them before.

A few years ago we were in the Republic of Slovenia on a ministry trip. (I wasn't totally sure where Slovenia was, but I got off the plane and they said it was Slovenia, so I took their word for it.) We stayed in a beautiful old hotel near a lake. It was right after Christmas and there was about a foot-and-a-half of snow everywhere. The lake was frozen over and people were skating on it. Everything we could see was absolutely beautiful.

But we couldn't see much of anything else because a fog had settled on the valley. Because of the fog, we couldn't see the most beautiful part of the surrounding area—the Alps. The mountain peaks were on a higher plane than we were, and they might as well not have been there at all, since we couldn't see them. For two days the fog covered the town, but on the third day it lifted. What we could see at that point—the world-famous Alps—had been there all along. But our vision had not been strong enough to penetrate the fog.

That is what happens when you start obeying Christ and get into His Word. The Bible begins to renew your mind. Your outward characteristics become transformed by His inner presence. And gradually, like the lifting of a fog, you begin to see things differently. You see what has been there all along—the victory and fulfillment in life that you have been seeking.

Becoming a
Biscuit for the Lord

God is baking you as a biscuit!

Now don't start searching your concordance to see where Scripture talks about believers being biscuits for the Lord. You won't find it. I confess up front that as a preacher from the South, who loves nothing better than a genuine Southern-style, melt-in-your-mouth biscuit, I've let my culture get the best of me. But I've found no better picture to describe a mysterious union that takes place between the believer and the Holy Spirit.

In Romans 12, as we've already discovered, the apostle Paul talks about yielding our lives as living sacrifices to Christ. That entire concept, to be understood completely, has to be linked with what he taught in Romans 6. Chapter 12 of Romans is a magnification of what is taught in chapter 6. In Romans 6:1 Paul says, "What shall we say then? Are we to continue in sin that grace might increase?" He knew that when some people hear the message of grace they hear the license to do whatever they want to do—to sin!

The group of people that Paul was writing to, the church in the ancient city of Rome, included what we would today call *antinomians. Anti* means "against."

Nomos means "law." The people were against law of any kind. Theological antinomians, whether then or now, believe they are so covered by the grace of God that the requirements of any law—scriptural, civil, or moral—do not apply to them. Thus you see Paul addressing all three categories of law in his epistle to them: moral (or "natural") law in Romans 1, civil law in Romans 13, and theological law in Romans 6. The Romans were the party lovers of the day. Their perspective was, "This is wonderful! We're under grace. We can do whatever we want to do. The more we sin, the more we help God out by giving His grace a reason to be showcased in our lives."

Paul squelches that argument in a hurry. He says in Romans 6:2, "May it never be! How shall we who died to sin still live in it?" I love those parking places that have a sign that says, "Don't even think about parking here." That's sort of what Paul is saying here: "You think God needs you to voluntarily sin more in order that His forgiveness can be shown more? Nice try, Romans, but don't even think about trying to win that argument!"

The text states, "May it never be!" Paul uses this phrase ten times in Romans to express his reaction to preposterous ideas that the Romans, or others, might entertain. He asks, "How shall we who died to sin still live in it?" This doesn't even sound reasonable, does it? Do you see why in Romans 12:1,2 Paul says that presenting yourself as a sacrifice to God is the only reasonable (logical) service? It simply is an unreasonable idea to think that someone who died to sin would then purposely continue in sin.

You are not going to start submitting yourself to Christ until you fully grasp the fact that you have become a new person. The old man has died. New Christians always struggle a bit at first to grasp this because it requires understanding the difference between the positional and the experiential parts of the Christian life. Positionally and "legally," God views believers as having died with Christ on Calvary's cross. When Christ died for us, it accomplished the same thing in God's sight as if *we* had died. Obviously we did not physically (experientially) die with Him on the cross. We weren't even alive at the time He died! But positionally, if we are trusting in Christ's death for the forgiveness of our sins, then when Christ died for those sins, we died to them as well. So now we have become new persons. We are born again to a new life in Christ. The challenge of the spiritual life is to see our *experience* more and more begin to reflect our *position*. If we have died to sin, why would we want to continue in sin?

United with Christ

Another way Paul describes our union with Christ is by the picture of baptism. He says in Romans 6:3, "Do you not know that all of us who have been baptized into Christ Jesus have been baptized into His death?" Here we see that something important has happened: We were immersed into Christ and His death. In the same way that one is immersed in and covered by water at baptism, so we are immersed and covered with the benefits of Christ's death. This is the baptism by the Spirit of God that Scripture refers to in 1 Corinthians 12:13.

Paul continues his teaching on our union with Christ in Romans 6:4: "Therefore we have been buried with Him through baptism into death, in order that as Christ was raised from the dead through the glory of the Father, so we too might walk in newness of life." Here we discover that not only were we identified with the *death* of Christ, but with His *life* as well. The word "newness" means "new life." When we understand these basic truths, they begin to motivate us to present our bodies as living sacrifices to Christ.

Romans 6:5 says, "For if we have become united with Him in the likeness of His death, certainly we shall be also in the likeness of His resurrection." When he says "united with," part of that Greek word is the little word *sun*, and is very significant to understand. *Sun* is the word that means "to be intimate with or inseparable from something." Another Greek word often translated "with" is *meta*, which is the "with of association." If I am in a room with a lot of people, that word would be *meta* because any of us could get up and leave at any given time. However, if something has been so united with me, and me with it, that it has become part of me, then that is the intimate word *sun*. It means something is inseparable from me. We have become inseparably united with Christ.

There is a union and an intimacy that is so thorough it is beyond separation. That is the union of the believer and Christ—united in death and united in life. So why would we decide to do our own thing and assert our own will? It really is preposterous, isn't it, to consider doing so. You can hear Paul crying out, "May it never be!" The very idea of being united with Christ in the payment of our sins, and then turning around and sinning more, defies both natural and supernatural reason. It is certainly not our "reasonable service of worship."

Biscuits for the Lord

With all due respect to my fellow believers who live outside the boundaries of the Southern states, I must take a moment to educate you on the finer points of "biscuitology." In doing so, you'll understand even better our union with Christ in His death and His life. In the South we make big biscuits. And we don't mean what you mean by "big." We're talking cat-head big! When was the last time you had a lightly browned, steaming hot, fluffy-on-the-inside, drenched-in-butter-and-sausage-drippings, gravy-coated biscuit the size of a cat's head? In the South, we don't think the day's worth pursuing if we don't start out with a basket of them at breakfast. And the day's definitely not worth talking about if we don't finish the day with a basket of them at supper.

Like most things in life, the best biscuits are those made simply: flour, shortening or butter, baking soda, salt, and milk. Complicate your recipe much beyond that and you're baking something besides biscuits. Now if we lay those five simple ingredients out on the counter, the ingredients are with each other on the counter, but they are still separate. *Meta* is the word Paul would use to describe their togetherness. But once we take those ingredients, mix them in a bowl, plop them out on a baking sheet, and subject them to the heat of the oven—well, now we're talking about *sun.* They are united together.

When those biscuits come out of the oven, you can no longer separate the milk from the flour from the salt from the baking soda. Those ingredients are so intimately intertwined with one another that both positionally (their actual blending) and experientially (that's the eating part) they are together. When you taste one of these marvels, you don't distinguish the salt from the milk. You are simply eating a biscuit. Both positionally and experientially, the union of the ingredients is complete.

Certainly no cook, no consumer, and not even a scientist could separate the original ingredients once they are baked. The ingredients are *sun* (with) each other. They are forever one! *Sun* is the part of word that comes in Romans 6:5: "For if we have become united *with* Him in the likeness of His death, certainly we shall be also in the likeness of His resurrection." The word translated "united with" is a compound word in Greek, made up of *sun* (with) and *phuo* (to produce or grow). Therefore we have been grown ("baked") together with Christ in His death and in His resurrection.

In other words, we are now biscuits for Jesus! Once you begin to realize that He has been baked into you, that His Spirit has been completely intermingled into your life from your head down to your toes, there is no possible way you could say the Spirit is here or the Spirit is there. He completely indwells you. Now that He lives in you, He does through you what you cannot do for yourself. Becoming a biscuit for the Lord is recognizing that He has been baked into you, and now you are to yield to Him because He came to do what you cannot do.

The Christian life is not me trying to be like Jesus. It is me allowing Jesus to be who He is in me. I can't go out and do anything I want to do anymore—a holy God has baked His Spirit into my life. He lives in me now. He controls me and enables me and lets me know when sin is present.

A New Creature in Christ

All kidding aside about biscuits, becoming a biscuit for the Lord is an expression I use to illustrate that we are new creatures in Christ, inseparably bound to Him forever. I find that very few believers are clear on the reality of their union with Christ. They simply have not grasped the reality that at every moment, because of their union with Christ in His death, they are freed from the condemnation and power of sin. And because of their union with Him in His resurrection, they have available the power of His life to live victoriously over sin. A dear little lady in Mississippi, now with the Lord, represents the best picture of these precious truths that I have ever seen.

At 84 years of age, she came to me when I was pastoring in Mississippi. She said, "Brother Wayne, you're the first person who ever told me that the Holy Spirit actually lives in me. You know, that is the most wonderful truth." She had come forward in an invitation that we had given in our church. That was on a Sunday. On Wednesday I saw her again and she looked worn-out. She had big, dark circles under her eyes. I said, "Are you okay? You look tired." She replied, "Oh, brother Wayne, I never realized God's life was in me. I've been living by myself all these years, but now that I know the Holy Spirit lives in me I've been up for the last three days and nights talking to Him. I've told Him everything that's been on my heart for a long time. I've talked His ears off now that I know I'm not alone anymore."

Isn't that wonderful? Dear friend, when was the last time you or I sat up all night, or even took an hour, to spend in fellowship with the Holy One with whom we are united? My precious friend was right—we are not alone anymore. The very Savior of the world lives in inseparable union with us if we have come to know Him as our Lord. If we have grown careless or callous about this wonderful truth, may God help us to walk in the reality of our union with Him. We have to become biscuits for Jesus. We must be aware of His life in us and how we are to be yielded to Him. When we realize that Christ is in us already, inseparably, then we will begin to echo the words of Paul about sin in the life of the believer: "May it never be!"

Christ
Is My Life

If you really want to understand how to allow Christ to live His life through you and give you victory over sin, you need to hear the testimony of someone who has been through the process personally—and successfully. And I know just the man!

In one of his letters in the New Testament, the apostle Paul gives ample instruction and illustration on how to yield to the lordship of Christ regardless of the situation. There is no degree of difficulty to which Paul could not relate. If Paul could allow Christ's victory over sin to become his own personal victory over sin, then we certainly can follow his example.

Did you know that when Paul wrote the New Testament letters of Philippians, Ephesians, Colossians, and Philemon he was in prison? And if you have ever read the letter to the Philippians, you know that one of its central themes is rejoicing in the Lord. How does one rejoice in the Lord when he or she is in prison? Philippians will tell us.

It all started when Paul went to Jerusalem to tell the exciting news of what God was doing in the Gentile world (the story begins in Acts 21). The general population of Jews in Jerusalem were not too excited about the news that

Paul was in town. They felt Paul was preaching against the temple and the Jewish faith. The leaders of the Jerusalem church told Paul to go down to the temple and demonstrate his cultural solidarity with Jewish people by participating in a ritual vow with several other Jewish men. They thought this would appease the Jews but when he went down to the temple, there were some Jews from Asia Minor who began stirring up the crowd with false accusations against Paul. They accused him of taking a Gentile beyond the wall of partition within the temple.

The result was a riot in the city, and Paul's life was saved only by the intervention of Roman soldiers. As a result of being arrested by the Romans, he ended up in prison at Caesarea for two years, and then was taken on to prison in Rome. He had been there over two years when he wrote the book of Philippians. As I mentioned, one of Paul's key themes in that book is joy, but I may surprise you by suggesting that joy and rejoicing are not the main themes. The key topic in the book of Philippians is the Lord Jesus Christ Himself. He is mentioned or discussed, in one way or another, at least 31 times in Philippians. It may now become immediately obvious what the connection is between Paul's prison position and his prison perspective. It was the *Christ connection.* It is when the Lord Jesus Christ was in proper perspective in Paul's life that joy and rejoicing came as a result. The same is true for us.

In Philippians 1:21 we read: "For to me, to live is Christ, and to die is gain." What in the world is Paul talking about? Here's the key: Where Paul was *physically* had nothing to do with his life, because *Christ was his life.* Granted, he was in prison, but he did not consider prison his life or his circumstance. *Christ* was his life and his circumstance. If God wanted him in prison, that was fine with Paul, because Christ had been a prisoner Himself once, hadn't He? How much confidence do you think Paul had that Jesus Christ would be able to live His life through the apostle while he was imprisoned? Probably a great deal of confidence for Paul knew that all he had to do was get out of the way (yield, surrender, submit) and the life of Christ would become apparent through him.

Freedom from Imprisonment

Before you decide that you really can't relate to Paul's experience in prison, you need to remember that not all prisons have walls or bars. You can be in all sorts of prisons today, every bit as confining as the one Paul was in. Perhaps you're imprisoned by unforgiveness. Perhaps by debt. Perhaps by loneliness, anger, fear, or depression. Before you dismiss Paul's experience as being irrelevant to you, I suggest you give him a hearing. You may discover that the freedom he gained behind bars might lead you to freedom as well. You must remember that Jesus Christ in you is not imprisoned by any of those things. If your attitude is focused on Christ, and you are yielded to Him, you will have His victory in your life in whatever circumstance you face.

One of the things I see in Philippians chapter 1 is that since Christ is Paul's life, prisons don't bother him. We see this in Philippians 1:12: "Now I want you to know, brethren, that *my circumstances have turned out for the greater progress of the gospel.*" I can just hear the people back in Philippi saying, "Poor old Paul. Bless his heart. He's in prison. O God, please get him out of prison." Paul writes back telling them, "I have something to tell you that you wouldn't know otherwise. I found here in prison a greater evangelism plan than I ever imagined. I thought I was going to come here and preach the gospel from a tent, but instead I've come as a prisoner. By allowing Christ to be Lord over these circumstances, some really interesting things are happening."

What were those exciting developments? He tells us in Philippians 1:13,14, that "my imprisonment in the cause of Christ has become well known throughout the whole praetorian guard and to everyone else, and that most of the brethren, trusting in the Lord because of my imprisonment, have far more courage to speak the word of God without fear." What he was saying was that God had orchestrated an amazingly effective evangelism strategy. Unbelievers were hearing the gospel and believers were being empowered to share the gospel. We often try all of our strategies for life, but it is interesting that when God orchestrates our lives and puts us into an imprisoned situation that we can't get out of, we learn what it means to be yielded to Jesus Christ. You may feel imprisoned in your marriage or your job, but by yielding to Christ, God uses our lives for a greater purpose than He can by any other method.

Look what Paul says in Philippians 4:22: "All the saints greet you, especially those of Caesar's household." God wanted Caesar's household to hear the gospel but had Paul gone the normal route, it would never have happened. So God sent him to a Roman prison, and as a result many people in Caesar's household became believers. That's what he's talking about. Christ is his life. Paul would never have planned things that way, but God had a plan that was far more effective.

Can you imagine Paul's imprisonment situation? The praetorian guards—big, stalwart men—had three round-the-clock shifts guarding Paul. They were on duty from three to eleven, eleven to seven, and seven to three. We don't know if the guards were chained to Paul (the words *imprisoned* and *chained* are the same word in Greek). We do know that Paul had a lot of flexibility. He could apparently entertain guests and write his letters. But we also know he was a political hostage. The Jews wanted him dead and the Romans didn't know what to do with him. Whether

Paul was literally in chains or not, it was guaranteed the Romans were not going to let him out of their sight. For the sake of argument, I think Paul was chained to his guards (we may have precedent for this in Acts 12:6).

At the end of the first shift, here comes this worn-out Roman soldier who has been chained to Paul for eight hours. He looks awful. He sees his buddy coming for the next shift and asks him who he's guarding.

The new guard says, "I have the guy named Paul. They call him the apostle Paul. He's probably a sissy."

This first guard looks at his buddy and says, "We're friends, aren't we?"

"Yeah, we're friends."

"Don't do it. Get your assignment changed. I promise you, you don't want to be chained to that man for eight hours."

"Oh, come on, man! I can handle a squirt like him."

"All right! But don't say I didn't warn you."

So the new guard walks into the cell. As soon as the chains are in place, Paul begins: "Well, glory! We only have a one-seat auditorium, and we have a packed house tonight! Now here's a piece of paper and a pencil. We are going to talk about the doctrine of soteriology tonight. Let's get on with the efficacy of the blood of Christ. Point number one: Jesus Christ is God's Son. Are you getting this?"

For eight hours that's all this guy hears. When he gets off his shift, as soon as he spots the new guard coming on duty he says, "Who do you have for your next shift?"

"I have that little wimpy guy named Paul."

"I'm warning you—don't go in there."

If things didn't happen exactly that way, it would not have been due to a lack of enthusiasm on Paul's part. This man was really the prisoner of the Lord, whether he was in jail or out of jail. It says in Ephesians that he wasn't a prisoner of the Jews. He wasn't a prisoner of the Romans.

He says in Ephesians 3:1 that he considered himself a prisoner of the Lord Jesus Christ.

The Attitude of Jesus

Philippians chapter 2 builds from chapter 1. Paul says, "Have this attitude in yourselves which was also in Christ Jesus" (Philippians 2:5). As a young believer I used to hear Philippians 2:6-9 preached frequently. It's a wonderful passage on how Christ emptied Himself of His glory and came down to this earth. He was willing to be submissive to His Father even unto death. That alone is a beautiful and powerful message. However, I don't recall ever hearing this passage preached in the context of Paul's imprisonment. The context is, "No matter what your circumstances are, have the same attitude as Christ Jesus, who came down to this earth and was willing to be humiliated and be a submissive person unto His Father, even unto death. And you should have this same attitude in yourselves."

It gets even better. Philippians 2:3,4 says, "Do nothing from selfishness or empty conceit, but with humility of mind let each of you regard one another as more important than himself; do not merely look out for your own personal interests, but also for the interests of others." When Christ is your life you are submitted to Him. Remember, you may be put in a prisonlike situation or relationship over which you have no control, but don't worry about it, because Christ is your circumstance. Now that you have a relationship with Him, if He is your life, *Christ* is your attitude. So people are not a threat to you anymore.

In chapter 1 of Philippians you discover that prisons don't bother you. And in chapter 2, people don't bother you. They become opportunities through which God can use you to serve Him. By serving Christ you end up serving people and loving them. There have been many times when I thought to myself, "If it weren't for people, I could live the Christian life." But I found out something: If it weren't for people, I would never even know what the Christian life is all about. It's *people* that drive me to the end of myself. When I discover that I can't truly love anyone with a self-less love in my own strength, then I am brought face-to-face with the need to surrender to the One who can love them through me.

When I first started pastoring at our church, the women's missionary group was preparing for its annual meeting. This is a forward-looking and energetic group that every year sets a new financial goal for missions involvement by the women in the churches in our denomination. Unfortunately, the goal-setting is not always easily accomplished, and I have memories of the squabbles and debates that would take place over priorities and commitments related to these budget processes.

On one particular night, I preached to the church from Philippians 2. I thought I had done a great job. I talked about how Paul sets forth Jesus as the example for believers, and how Paul mentions Timothy and Epaphroditus as models of godly servants whom he wants the Philippians to observe. The whole chapter is about being a servant for Christ. But at the conclusion of the service my whole message seemed to have gotten lost. I was confronted by the leader of the women's missionary group over an offering that we were supposed to be taking. Matters concerning the amount to ask for, the approach to take, and other things were swirling in a political fashion.

Driving home, I found myself in more and more of a confrontational mood. Here I had preached my heart out on servanthood, only (in my humble opinion) to be nailed by the women's leader over what I thought were trivial financial matters. I began to strategize about how to get back at the woman. Isn't it funny how we do that? I was thinking, "'Vengeance is mine,' saith Wayne." I was thinking about all the things I could say to her to get her back because of her "attack" upon me. I was upset, and I was angry. In fact, I had asked her, "What was the goal for this offering last year?"

"Thirteen hundred dollars."

"What's the goal this year?"

"Thirteen hundred and fifty dollars."

"Do you think God can afford 50 more dollars?" What I was really saying was, "Why put *your* goal on God? Why not let God do it His own way?" It wasn't good. We both had the wrong attitude.

On the way home I started having a little pity party. Every pity party I've ever thrown has had only one person on the guest list: Wayne Barber. Pity parties are the loneliest parties on earth, and they make the host feel even more sorry for himself. I began to think about how badly she had treated me, and what I was going to say back to her. And then it was as if those verses I had just preached started coming back to me. God was saying, "Wayne, do you love this woman?"

"Absolutely not, Lord! I don't even *like* this woman." (I might be tempted to lie to you, but I'm not going to lie to Him.)

"Wayne, I want you to make a choice to love her," God said. "And in the meantime, since you're so worried about your church being under a legalistic goal of $1350, I want you to give the $1350."

Again, I first thought, "'Get away from me, Satan!' This couldn't be God. This would take two miracles: one, for me to even *get* $1350; and two, for me to be persuaded to give it to this particular group! No way was God in this."

But the more I thought about it, the more I knew I was hearing the convicting voice of God. By the time I got home, I had made the choice to obey the voice of the Spirit.

Many times people get in the twilight zone when it comes to hearing the voice of God. How do you know the Holy Spirit of God has spoken to you? Just let me say one thing right here: The more time you spend in the Word of God, the more sensitive you become to His voice. My mother has been with the Lord in heaven for 17 years. Yet if the phone rang today, and she began to speak, I'd say, "Hello, mom!" She might say back to me, "Wayne, how did you know it was me? We haven't spoken for 17 years." I'd say, "Come on, mom. I spent so much time with you when you were here that I'd recognize your voice anywhere." That's the way it is. The more time you spend in the Word of God, the more easily you will recognize the Spirit of God's voice when He speaks to you. It may not be audibly, but you will sense the convicting hand of God upon your heart.

When I arrived home, I called the church treasurer. He thought I had lost my mind. I told him, "I'm going to give $1350 for missions; however, I want it to be done anonymously." He was willing to work with me. The following Sunday morning I got up with much joy in my heart. Both miracles had occurred. The Lord had provided the funds for me to give, and He had given me a genuine desire to serve the women by giving it to their missions effort. I said to the lady who was in charge of the program, "The Lord has provided the funds. Now you can move ahead as the Lord wants you to." I saw that precious lady's mouth just drop open, since the last time we had discussed this I had not been very supportive. That year our church gave more than we have ever given before to that particular offering because a spirit of confrontation had been replaced by a spirit of liberty and freedom in Christ.

As a result of that experience, God began to create within me a joy in serving and loving her. As a matter of fact, I began to see her sense of humor. Before, I had been so narrowly focused on my own agenda that I could not even see it. Suddenly I began to realize that she was a person of great worth. Over the years we have become dear friends. Now that I have known her for 16 years, she is probably one of the dearest people to me in our church. It is amazing how Christ can knit relationships together when we let His attitude replace our own. When we are willing to realize that He is our life, then we also realize He is our attitude as well. We know we have surrendered our sword to Him when we have liberty and freedom in serving other people.

The Upward Call of God

In chapter 1 of Paul's epistle to the Philippians, he says, "*Christ is my life*," so the prison is not getting me down. In chapter 2 he says, "*Christ is my attitude*," so even the people around me are opportunities for me to share the gospel of Christ.

However, many people stumble when they get to chapter 3. In that chapter he says, "*Christ is my goal.*" In Philippians 3:14 we read, "I press on toward the goal for the prize of the upward call of God in Christ Jesus." This is unique for Paul, given his background. Prior to his conversion he was a person who was a great man of religion in Israel. Of anyone who ever understood religion and the works of man for God, Paul stands out. As a matter of fact, he gives his pedigree later in chapter 3.

But he writes in Philippians 3:1, "Finally, my brethren, rejoice in the Lord. To write the same things again is no trouble to me, and it is a safeguard for you." That has always encouraged me because many times I am afraid to repeat myself. I am finding from the apostle Paul that he had to repeat himself over and over again. In verses 2 and 3 he says, "Beware of the dogs, beware of the evil workers, beware of the false circumcision; for we are the true circumcision, who worship in the Spirit of God and glory in Christ Jesus and put no confidence in the flesh."

Religion puts all its confidence in the flesh. But when you have a relationship with Christ, you have a true circumcision of the heart. It is not of the flesh anymore; it is of the heart. We are to put *no confidence* in the flesh. Paul was a man who underwent a radical transformation. He once was a man who thought he could do it all for God, but now he realizes that he can put no confidence in his human abilities. He says in Philippians 3:4-7, "Although I myself might have confidence even in the flesh. If anyone else has a mind to put confidence in the flesh, I far more: circumcised the eighth day, of the nation of Israel, of the tribe of Benjamin, a Hebrew of Hebrews; as to the Law, a Pharisee; as to zeal, a persecutor of the church; as to the righteousness which is in the Law, found blameless. But whatever things were gain to me, those things I have counted as loss for the sake of Christ."

Religion to many people brings great gain. They are lost and don't even know Christ, but they are religious, and in that they find great gain. It gives them help in political arenas, and perhaps in their business and social contacts. But Paul says, "Those things that were gain to me I have counted as loss for Christ." In Philippians 3:8,9 he says, "More than that, I count all things to be loss in view of the surpassing value of knowing Christ Jesus my Lord, for whom I have suffered the loss of all things, and count them but rubbish in order that I may gain Christ, and may be found in Him, not having a righteousness of my own derived from the Law, but that which is through faith in Christ, the righteousness which comes from God on the basis of faith."

Unless we put our faith in Christ (which means we are submissive, obedient, and surrendered to what His Word tells us to do), then we do not yet understand what it means to live the Christ life. But when we put our faith in

Him, it is Christ in us—our attitude, our life, our goal. Paul rounds out the whole book when he says in Philippians 4:13, "I can do all things through Him who strengthens me." In other words, *Christ is my strength.* There is nothing in life that can overwhelm me now because Christ lives in me. I'm a biscuit for Jesus, fully in union with Him.

That's why I can live this Christian life. If I can simply absorb what the Scriptures say, and observe how people in Scripture lived, the message is the same, over and over: I *am in union with Jesus Christ, and I am allowing His Word to dominate my life.* I must be willing to confess and repent when I am wrong. I must be willing to surrender to whatever His Word says. When I do that, Christ is free to take over, and He begins to do through me what I could never have done myself.

Boasting in the Lord

Paul used to boast in himself. For years he boasted about what he could do for God. He even said in Philippians 3, "According to the Law, I was found blameless." That is a boast. No man ever stood before the law blameless except Jesus Christ. The law he was talking about had to be the traditions of the Jewish elders, the Pharisees, who added their own rules and regulations to God's law. The laws (traditions) that the Pharisees came up with were written by them in such a way that a person could possibly keep them. They had to do with external rules, rituals, and regulations, not with the heart.

One day Jesus was teaching when one of the Pharisees walked by. Jesus pointed at him and said, "Except your righteousness *exceed* that of the Pharisees, you will never enter the kingdom of God." That is a powerful statement. Paul used to be one of those that Jesus was talking about. Then he met Jesus on the Damascus road, and in the next several years Paul got straightened out on the difference between law and grace. In Philippians, Paul demonstrates that righteousness does not come by what we can do for God. Righteousness comes only by faith in what God has done for us in Christ.

Paul said, "Therefore in Christ Jesus I have found reason for boasting in things pertaining to God" (Romans 15:17). He has a brand-new form of boasting. You have to know the other side of Paul to recognize this marvelous change that came over him. He continues, "For I will not presume to speak of anything except what Christ has accomplished through me, resulting in the obedience of the Gentiles by word and deed" (Romans 15:18). Paul only speaks of the things that Christ has done in and through his life. He used to speak of what he could do for God. Now he would never open his mouth unless it glorified Christ.

Have you and I fallen victim to the same boasting that Paul had? Oh, we may not boast outwardly, but do we boast inwardly? Do we think that God has gotten the better part of the deal, that the kingdom has increased in stature by our presence in it? Philippians will help us see that all such boasting is vanity. All we have to boast in is the Lord Jesus Christ and what He has promised to do in and through us. This is the Christ life. This is the Christian life.

Bondservants
of Jesus

American history, unfortunately, has so sullied our thinking about servanthood that it is next to impossible to grasp the strength of this biblical metaphor. One of the most beautiful pictures in Scripture is that of servanthood. Today when we in America hear the word "servant," our mind automatically recoils against the atrocities of nineteenth-century slavery. And "atrocities" is saying it mildly. Though the words "slave" or "servant" occur in the Scriptures, they in no way parallel or support the degrading and dehumanizing practices perpetrated upon millions of Africans who were forced against their wills to be someone's slave.

And therein lies the key word: "forced." In the biblical concept of servanthood, the will of the servant is at the heart of the matter. Becoming a bondservant of Jesus Christ—by choice—provides yet another graphic illustration of the Christ life.

In Romans 1:1 Paul begins his letter this way: "Paul, a *bondservant* of Christ Jesus, called as an apostle, set apart for the gospel of God." Notice the three ways Paul identifies himself in this one verse: He is a bondservant of Christ, one called as an apostle, and one set apart for the gospel. The last two designations were, in a manner of speaking, done "to" Paul, not things he did to himself. He didn't call himself or set himself apart. Those were states in which Paul's will was passive and God's was active. But the first characteristic, his bondservanthood, is a different story. And you have to understand how he became a bondservant in order to understand the role of the will. God doesn't force anyone to become His bondservant. But if you and I are wise, we will follow Paul into that sacred position.

Does even the thought of volunteering for slavery get the hair up on the back of your neck? Do you feel a little resistance—maybe even a lot of resistance—to the idea of choosing to be a slave? Don't worry about it. It's just your upbringing talking to you. You and I have been so conditioned to think that slavery is bad, the lowest rung on the ladder of social civility, that we react negatively. But don't forget that God is not an American. His idea of slavery is not what you've read about in your history books. As with everything, we need to read about it first in Scripture.

The first thing you have to deal with when it comes to dying to self is your will—what you want versus what God wants. You have to say, "I want what God wants." When you can come to that place, then you are beginning to make giant strides toward dying to self. You must choose God's will over your own will. The word for bondservant is *doulos*, which means "a slave." We think of a slave as someone who works because he *has* to.

But Paul is saying he is a love slave. He does what he does not because he has to, but because he *gets* to! When we come to understand that the Christian life is something that I "get to do," not something I "have to do," then we are coming near to the Christ life.

Bondservants by Choice

Think about how most people get into the Christian life. They are raised by parents who spend most of their time telling them "No!" about various and sundry lifestyle choices. As young adults, they look back regretfully thinking, "I never got to do such and such when I was growing up," as if they were being prevented from enjoying some of life's legitimate opportunities. Having become believers along the way, they carry this same mentality into their relationship with God, resigning themselves to thinking that obeying God is just the adult version of obeying their parents (don't get me wrong—in some ways it is). Most adult Christians are willing to pay the price of drabness and boredom which (in their ill-informed minds) come with Christianity in order to avoid going to hell. In other words, "I guess I have to obey God in order to stay out of hell and get into heaven. I don't like the deal, but I don't have much of a choice." If that's the version of the "Good News" we're spreading, no wonder we don't seem to see as many people come to Christ as we'd like!

In actuality, the biblical version of the Good News (the gospel) is much better. To cut to the chase, why do you think someone like the apostle Paul would exchange everything he had (those things listed in Philippians 3) for what he got (the hard things Paul lists in 2 Corinthians 6 and 11)—and do it voluntarily? There must be more to this than we know about. Let's see exactly how a person came to be a bondservant in biblical times.

Deuteronomy 15:12-17 says, "If your kinsman, a Hebrew man or woman, is sold to you, then he shall serve you six years, but in the seventh year you shall set him free. And when you set him free, you shall not send him away empty-handed. You shall furnish him liberally from your flock and from your threshing floor and from your wine vat; you shall give to him as the LORD your God has blessed you. And you shall remember that you were a slave in the land of Egypt, and the LORD your God redeemed you; therefore I command you this today. And it shall come about if he says to you, 'I will not go out from you,' because he loves you and your household, since he fares well with you, then you shall take an awl and pierce it through his ear into the door, and he shall be your servant forever. And also you shall do likewise to your maidservant."

Doesn't exactly sound like the slavery that we're used to picturing, does it? There were several reasons one Hebrew might become indentured to another: to pay off a debt, or if the person had no other means of support due to the loss of his immediate family. If he did become the servant of another person, he was to be treated well during the six years of service which the law required, and then be set free. And when he was given his freedom, he was to be loaded down with supplies from the master's flocks and fields. This generosity was to be a perpetual reminder of how God had blessed Israel by giving them the goods of the Egyptians when they were freed from their 400 years of bondage in Egypt.

Now comes the part of the arrangement that demonstrates the uniqueness of biblical "slavery." It was entirely possible that, during his period of servanthood, the indentured Hebrew had been treated so well by his master that he had developed a heart of love toward the master and his family. In fact, a servant might realize that he would be far better off being a servant in the master's household than he would be out fending for himself. But note that it is not just material prosperity that is the issue, although that is mentioned in the passage. It is *love* that is the issue: "It shall come about if he says to you, 'I will not go out from you,' because he loves you and your household, since he fares well with you. . . ."

In other words, the slave says, "Where am I going to go? Nobody has ever treated me like you treat me." He is doing well with his master, and he does not want to leave. Remember the disciples saying, "Lord, if we leave You, where will we go?"

Once freed from the obligation to his master, if a servant made a choice to remain with the master, the decision would be ratified publicly. In this public proclamation, it would be noted that the servant was *making a choice based on his freedom of will.* As a permanent sign of that choice, a small puncture was made in the ear, the scar of which would identify the servant as a bondservant by choice. Nobody was forcing the servant to choose. Out of love for one's master, the choice was made publicly to become and remain a servant. Thus a servant became a bondservant, or a *doulos.*

For Paul, calling himself a bondservant of Christ meant that his will now had now been submitted to the will of his master, the One who called him and set him apart for the gospel. It was Paul's own free choice to deny anything that he could accomplish in life on his own, and instead submit to Christ's will. This is the first step in dying to self. You have to deal with your will.

Embracing God's Agenda

Along with this comes dying to your agenda. As a bondservant, whose agenda would you be living by—yours or your master's? When you submit your will, you also submit everything that would ever be a manifestation of your will. When you pull out your scheduler or planner and look at your agenda for the day, what does that agenda reflect? It reflects your will. You choose the appointments and activities that fill your day. But as a bondservant, you can have no agenda except the agenda of your Master. But don't worry—God is not going to be dictating your day to you. Bondservants in biblical times were sort of given the run of the master's house and affairs. The master and his servants were trusted friends (see John 15:15). The master set the overall agenda but allowed the servants to work out the details.

When you die to self, all the soulish agenda has to go. Romans 1:9 says, "For God, whom I serve in my spirit. . . ." What does Paul mean by serving in his spirit? He has identified himself as a bondservant, and now appears to be saying that the realm of his service is first *in the spirit.*

Theologians differ on the makeup of humans. There is a "dichotomous view" of man and a "trichotomous view" of man. The dichotomous view says that man is made up of two parts: material (body) and immaterial (soul or spirit). The trichotomous view says that man is made up of three parts: a material part (body) and two immaterial parts (soul and spirit). People have asked me at times if I hold to a dichotomous or a trichotomous view of man. My answer usually doesn't satisfy them: It depends on which text of Scripture you look at because both views seem to be supported in Scripture.

When it comes to our walk with God, it becomes very apparent that we are trichotomous. First Thessalonians 5:23 says, "Now may the God of peace Himself sanctify you entirely; and may your spirit and soul and body be preserved complete, without blame at the coming of our Lord Jesus Christ." Hebrews 4:12 says, "For the word of God is living and active and sharper than any two-edged sword, and piercing as far as the division of soul and spirit, of both joints and marrow, and able to judge the thoughts and intentions of the heart."

Both Paul and the author of Hebrews, at least in these two passages, draw a line between the soul and the spirit. When Paul says, "whom I serve in my spirit," he means he is not serving God with soulish desires. He has been set free from that. He says in 2 Timothy 1:3, "I thank God, whom I serve with a clear conscience." The word "clear" in that verse should actually be "cleansed," a cleansed conscience. Cleansed of what? Cleansed of the soulishness that usually degrades our conscience. Paul serves God now freely in the spirit. There is nothing soulish that is hanging on to him.

So those who hold to the trichotomous view of man seem to be on good ground when they suggest that the soul is the "carnal" part of man and the spirit is the "spiritual" part of man. Every person has a soul (mind, will, emotions), but the spirit of man is made alive by God's Holy Spirit at the time of our conversion. In that sense, then, Paul is saying that he is setting aside his soulish agenda—what he might want to do—and serving God out of the spirit with a cleansed conscience. No guilt, no struggle, no fighting with God—just service in the spirit which is then manifested in the external actions of his life.

If you have dealt with your will, you no longer have an agenda. You can say, "God, I'm going to serve You whether You heal me or not. God, I'm going to serve You whether You make me rich or not. There are no strings attached. I'm going to serve You not because I *have to* but because I *want to.*" When you can say that, you know you have offered your agenda to Him.

Whose Agenda?

Years ago, while pastoring a church, I wanted the church to buy a piece of land out in the middle of nowhere and develop it for ministry purposes. I was thinking, "Here we are in the poorest county of the United States. The demographics are ripe for ministry: 89 percent minority population, poverty, poor education." I had found a camp of several hundred acres for sale. I had always had a vision, or should I say "agenda" for starting a camp, and I was always trying to get God to bless my vision. I was always helping God out because I thought He was so busy that He needed me to help Him create new visions for ministry.

I found out you could buy the land and then sell the timber rights for more than the land cost! You would never have to make a payment on the land. It would pay for itself. It had deer all over the place, and also a 17-acre lake full of bass. (Now, mind you, those deer and those bass had nothing to do with my vision. They were just icing on the cake.) This was going to be a place for ministry. The camp was already built—California redwood buildings, a swimming pool, all the stuff was already there. I just knew God was in this, and that once our church's deacons saw this property, they would be singing my praises for having such a grand vision for ministry.

So I took the deacons out to see the land. We looked at maps. We walked around the buildings. We looked at the swimming pools and the lake. We surveyed the timber that would so easily pay for the whole thing. Knowing they were probably ready to sign on the dotted line, I said, "So what do you think?" The deacons, to a man, said to one another, "I don't want to deal with this. Do you want to deal with this? I don't think this is what we're supposed to do." In about five minutes my whole vision was destroyed. I went home thinking, "These people don't have enough vision to get in out of the rain."

Well, that weekend, Roy Hession, who wrote *The Calvary Road*, was sitting at my kitchen table with me. Roy had become like a father to me, and I poured out my heart to him—which, looking back, was not a pretty sight. I told him the story about the camp and the vision-impaired deacons. In as humble a way as possible, I made the deacons look as bad as I possibly could and made myself look as spiritual as I possibly could.

After I finished my tale of woe, Roy said quietly, "Wayne, you just don't get it, do you? You have to die to your vision so God can raise up His vision in your life. You have never learned how to die to your agenda and live unto God's."

He was right. We have not truly died to self until we have dealt with our will, our agenda, and our attitude. Paul said, "I am under obligation both to Greeks and to barbarians, both to the wise and to the foolish" (Romans 1:14). The word "barbarian" here is not referring to cannibals but to those who did not enjoy the education and sophistication of the Greek culture. It's interesting that in 1 Corinthians 1 Paul says that what the world considers wise is actually foolish in God's sight, even as what the barbarians thought was wise was probably foolish in the Greeks' sight.

I was in Greece several years ago speaking at the foot of Mount Olympus on the Aegean Sea, and momentarily I forgot that I was preaching to people who spoke Greek. When I began explaining the nuances of two Greek words from the New Testament, *zoe* and *bios*, they began to snicker. My Tennessee drawl had put a barbarian's spin on the Greek pronunciation of the words. They good-naturedly called me "Wayne the Barbarian" the rest of the week because I appeared so uneducated to them in their own language. Sometimes that must be how our agendas appear to God. We put our own spin, our own pronunciation, our own interpretation, on what we think He is doing in the world, and the comparison is about like a barbarian walking into a Greek temple—a little out of place, to say the least. We have to give up the agenda of our flesh for the agenda of the kingdom of God.

We Owe Everything to God

In verse 14 of Romans 1 Paul says, "I'm a debtor. I'm under obligation." This is not a contradiction of his freewill choice to be a bondservant of Christ. This is a matter of loyalty on Paul's part. Once he had chosen to "indenture" himself to Christ, He was obligated to carry out the Master's will. He did not feel the Lord owed him something. Instead, he felt he owed the Lord everything. Many European countries, and America as well, have become mired in an imploding welfare system that says, "I deserve something." The more people are given something for nothing, the fewer there are to produce what the welfare system gives out. Paul believed that if you were going to become a bondservant of God, then you lived in dependence on Him. He has promised to meet our every need as His servants. No one "owes" us anything. In reality, we owe everything to the Master because of what He has done for us. This truth is what begins to shape the attitude of gratitude.

These three areas—our will, our agenda, our attitude—are what we must major on when it comes to dying to self. I've dealt with my will, which means I've dealt with my agenda, which means I've dealt with my attitude. I'm not doing this because I have to. I'm doing this because I get to. It is a love choice, made in complete freedom, which I make every time I come to one of life's intersections (such as a teeming-with-deer-and-bass, fully-equipped, potentially-paid-for camp facility). These "intersections" are very normal and innocent events that we experience daily. In fact, they are opportunities to reach up and feel that little scar on our ear that reminds us of our chosen role.

Paul said, "I glory in the cross of Christ alone" (Galatians 6:14). By this he meant that he found his identity in the cross. Our identity is not in what we do or in what we think we are. Our identity is that we are believers in (bondservants of) Jesus Christ. The word for "glory" is *doxa*, which means the "recognition" or "worth" of something. Your worth and my worth can only be found at the cross, where we died in union with Christ. When we are willing to die to ourselves and our agenda, as Paul illustrated in the book of Philippians, then we can glory in the cross. Then all our glory will be pointed toward Him and not toward us.

Paul also said that there were enemies of the cross of Christ (Philippians 3:18). The people who are not willing to surrender to Christ in the twentieth century are enemies of the cross of Christ. Until we are willing to take our place with Him on the cross and find our identity not in ourselves but in Him, then we cannot glory in the cross. Instead, we live by trying to escape the cross. By doing so we become enemies of the cross. Most doctrine gets off-centered when people don't understand the importance of the cross in the life of the believer.

In Jeremiah 9:23 the prophet identifies what enemies of the cross love to boast about: "Thus says the Lord, 'Let not a wise man boast of his wisdom, and let not the mighty man boast of his might, let not a rich man boast of his riches.'" Even in religious circles, we love to boast in what we know and what we can do. Dr. Vance Havner used to say, "We've got the M.Ds, the Ph.Ds, the D.Ds, and the Th.Ds. To me they're all a bunch of fiddle-dee-dees." We are dying by degrees because we like to glory in what we know.

Dr. Spiros Zodhiates, a member of our church and a tremendous scholar of the biblical languages, and with whom I participated in a radio and television ministry for a decade, challenged me one Sunday after I had preached. I was excited about what I had shared from a passage, and he came up to me after the service and said, "Wayne, I'd like to talk to you about that verse."

"Why, did I miss it?"

"Oh, no," he replied, "you didn't miss it. You really didn't get close enough to claim a miss!"

Immediately God was loving me by showing me what I didn't know. You can boast in what your strength is, but if you do, be ready to be humbled, because you probably aren't as strong as you think you are. Have you ever heard of the fellow who survived the great Johnstown Flood of 1889? He couldn't wait to get to heaven to share his testimony. When he got to heaven he said to Saint Peter, "I've got to share my testimony. I survived the Johnstown flood." He began to pester Saint Peter to death, and finally, Peter said, "All right! All right! We're having a testimony meeting on Friday. You can speak right after Noah."

In Jeremiah 9:24 God tells us what we are supposed to boast about: "'But let him who boasts boast of this, that he understands and knows Me, that I am the LORD who exercises lovingkindness, justice, and righteousness on earth; for I delight in these things,' declares the LORD." The only glorying we have is in the Lord Jesus Christ. He is our strength, our knowledge, and our wisdom. First Corinthians 1:30,31 says, "By His doing you are in Christ Jesus, who became to us wisdom from God, and righteousness and sanctification and redemption, that, just as it is written, 'Let him who boasts, boast in the Lord.'" Christ is the treasure house of wisdom and knowledge. All the riches we have are because of him.

Reach up and touch your ear. Do you feel the mark of the bondservant of God? If not, it may be time for you, as an act of your will, to give yourself back to Him in service from this point forward. All you've got to lose is a stubborn will and a self-serving agenda. And where have they gotten you so far?

The Rest *of* Grace

9

A New Attitude
Toward Scripture

For recreation, my wife and I like to go out driving. It's just something we enjoy doing—especially if we can stop somewhere and eat. As a matter of fact, driving and eating out have become our favorite sports. One beautiful afternoon as we were riding along I noticed that my wife was being very quiet. It bugs me when she does that because I start wondering what she's thinking.

We stopped at a stoplight, and I said, "What are you thinking?"

"I'm not thinking anything."

I knew she was thinking something. When we got to the next stoplight I said, "Come on, I know you're thinking something."

"I'm not thinking anything."

By the fifth stoplight we had become upset with each other because she would not tell me what she was thinking. Why would any husband want to know what his wife thinks? The answer is simple: I love my wife; therefore, I love to know what she thinks. How am I going to please her if I don't know what she thinks?

It is amazing to me how many people say they love Jesus but don't have time to find out what He thinks.

Translation? They don't have time for His Word. That's where you find out what God thinks. That's where you find out what God wants. How can we please Him if we don't know His Word?

Of course, Satan will do everything he can to keep you from your Bible. The devil is cornered and knows his time is short, so he wants to be spreading his lies and entrapping people in hell, and the last thing he wants is to let anyone spend time with the truth. He is lashing out with all his demonic angels to pull believers off the path of surrender to Jesus Christ.

It sort of reminds me of a cat we used to have. His name was Alexander the Great, though there wasn't anything great about him. I don't like cats much, since I'm allergic to cats and cats are allergic to work, but this cat was particularly sorry. He probably weighed 15 pounds, and all he did was sit around and shed hair on everything.

One day I was lying on the sofa watching a ball game when I heard a terrific animal cry. It sounded like something was dying, so I leaped onto the porch to catch the action. Fritz, our neighbor's boxer, had come into our yard and cornered our cat. Even though I didn't like our cat very much, I didn't see why it needed to be torn apart by some neighbor's dog, so I started rooting for him. I think I shouted something like, "Come on, you mangy cat, do something positive for once in your sorry life!"

As Fritz moved in for the kill, Alexander the Great earned his nickname. He leaped onto that dog's face and dug in. The dog tried to shake him off, but that just made it worse. Our cat hung on for dear life, just shredding that old bulldog's face. I'd never heard such sounds of pain before! Finally the dog got him off and ran home, yelping in anguish. The cat pranced around the yard as if to say, "Okay, big boy, you want some more?" That dog never bugged our cat again—he would come over to the property line, but he wouldn't cross it.

When Alexander was cornered, he did his most damage. That's exactly how Satan is reacting in our world today. He knows his time is limited, he is lurking about to seek whom he may devour, and above all he wants to keep people from the truth. The devil doesn't want us reading our Bibles, because he knows the impact that truth can have on our lives.

The Secret to Spiritual Intimacy

We've been talking in this book about the Christ life—about surrendering, yielding, and submitting our lives to Christ. When a person lives the Christ life, he or she will begin to see God's Word from a totally different perspective. The Bible will stop being a book you "have to read" and become a book you "get to read." Why? Because it's how you grow in intimacy with the One to whom you are surrendered. It's how you learn to distinguish His voice from the voice of your flesh. I'm told that the U.S. Treasury trains investigators to recognize counterfeit money by exposing them continually to the real thing. Then when they see a counterfeit bill, it stands out from what they've been concentrating on and they spot it instantly. The same is true of God's voice. When you fill your heart and mind with His Word, any counterfeit word that comes along—whether from you, another person, or the devil himself—will stand out like a sore thumb.

In 2 Timothy 3:16,17 the apostle Paul encouraged his young protégé, Timothy, to depend on the Word of God for everything: "All Scripture is inspired by God and profitable for teaching, for reproof, for correction, for training in righteousness; that the man of God may be adequate, equipped for every good work."

One of the things this verse reveals is that Scripture is God-breathed—right out of the mouth of God. That's what the words "inspired by God" mean. Those three words are actually an English rendering of one Greek word, *theopneustos*. *Theo* is from *theos*, meaning "God," and *pneustos* is an adjectival form from the verb *pneo*, "to blow." So the compound word in Greek means "breathed by God." Where does breath originate? It originates from the "breather," who in this case is God Himself. God breathed, or animated, His words for mankind the same way He breathed life into the first man, Adam (Genesis 2:7). Though He used man to *pen* the words, God Himself *breathed* the words.

How Can I Best Obey?

There is a point you reach in your walk with God when one day you discover that you have stopped questioning what the Bible says. I don't know how or when it happens; I only know that it does. From that point on in your life your question for God is not, "Do I have to obey this?" but "How can I best obey this?" When we love God, we want to read what He has spoken to us.

The word "profitable" in 2 Timothy 3:16 does not mean "materialistically profitable" but "profitable to our spiritual life." It means that the Word is useful, beneficial, rewarding, and helpful to us in a number of ways.

1. The Word teaches us. If you are concerned about your spiritual life and want Christ to be who He should be in your life, then you have to be taught correctly. There is truth concerning God, and you must know it. This is foundational in any endeavor in life. How will His Word profit you? *It will clarify in your mind how God really sees things.*

If I have trouble in my family, I have to go to the Word of God. God has the design for the family, and it is in His Word. If I have trouble in my finances, I have to go to the Word of God. God sets the standard for how we should manage our finances.

We could go on and on, but here's the point: The Bible doesn't present a list of formulas for living life. It doesn't cover every realm of knowledge and practice known to man. But the primary areas of the spiritual life which it does discuss—plus all the other insights it offers about life from God's perspective—are the truth. It has been said that not all truth is in the Bible, but everything in the Bible is truth.

2. *The Word reproves us.* The word "reproof" is the idea of "exposing something." It is also translated "conviction." It is the word we find in John 3:19,20 when John says, "And this is the judgment, that the light is come into the world, and men loved the darkness rather than the light; for their deeds were evil. For everyone who does evil hates the light, and does not come to the light, lest his deeds should be *exposed.*" The Word of God will expose our sin when we are wrong. It will show us where we are off track.

3. *The Word corrects us.* The Bible can get us back on track. The word for "correction" is the same word for setting broken bones, or anything that is out of order. Doesn't it stand to reason that anyone who makes something knows how to fix it? Of course. And God can put our lives back together when they get out of sorts.

4. *The Word trains us in righteousness.* This word comes from the word *paideia* which means "child training." The concept here is that, over time, training takes place which changes the trainee. The Word of God will train us as a child is trained if we will allow it.

The Word of God is profitable first of all for teaching, for clarification. Is teaching enough? No. With the teaching we understand, but we are reproved when we go away from that understanding. Then we are brought back to that understanding by correction. If we continue to repeat the process over and over again, we can say that we have been trained in righteousness.

Have you ever told your young child not to go out in the street and play? You think the child understands and that you did a great job teaching him. He is a well-taught child. One day you look for him out in the yard. Where is he? In the middle of the street. You thought he had been taught, but that is not where learning ends. You must reprove him with what you've taught him. You say, "Here's what I taught you to do. You didn't do it. Here's the consequence for it." You correct him. You show him again what to do. You think he understands this time. He's been taught. He's been reproved. He's been corrected. You look out the window 30 minutes later. Where is he? In the middle of the street. You go back and get him. This happens over and over again.

Finally one day you think, "Oh, no. I forgot to tell him not to go out into the street today." So you look out the window, but lo and behold there he is in the yard playing. What has happened? He was taught all along, but now he is *trained* by the teaching, the reproof, and the correction. That's what the Word of God will do in the life of the one submitted to it.

Transformed by the Word

What exactly is all this training for? What is the purpose or the goal of teaching, reproof, correction, and training? Second Timothy 3:17 says, "That the man of God may be adequate, equipped for every good work." This is an important verse. Unfortunately, we hear verse 16 quoted far more frequently than verse 17. There is a *purpose* for being taught, reproved, corrected, and trained. It is so that we, God's people, can be adequate for every good work.

Let me ask you a question: What is the first thing we do with most Christians when they enter the kingdom of God? Do we put them into the Word or do we put them into the work? My experience has been that 99.9 percent of the time we put them right into work. Have they been taught? No. Have they been reproved? No. Have they been corrected? No. Have they been trained? Certainly not. Therefore, they grow as a believer thinking that "works" are what the Christian life is all about.

Of course, good works are important. Verse 17 says that is the ultimate goal of our training. But consider this: Would anyone in any other endeavor or vocation in the world be put on the job without training? Of course not! It only results in lost time, lost production, and lost profits. Lost profits—didn't verse 16 say that the Word of God is profitable? Indeed it is. And yet we fail to teach, reprove, correct, and train new believers adequately by getting them into the Word before we get them into the work. Should we be surprised when, down the road, they don't become spiritually profitable (mature) believers? Ephesians 2:10 says, "For we are His workmanship, created in Christ Jesus for good works, which God prepared beforehand, that we should walk in them." It is obvious that God wants us to walk profitably in His good works.

So we develop a brand-new perspective on the Word of God when we start submitting to Christ. Now since you love Him you want to know what He says, for by knowing what He says you will then know how to please Him. We have the Spirit living in us and enabling us to get into the Word. We get into the Word for a different reason than ever before—it is not just for knowledge, not just for information, but for *transformation.*

It is interesting how many people say, "I just love Jesus." Yet when you get around them for awhile, you find they are not consistently reading and studying the Word of God. Jesus said, "He who has My commandments and keeps them, he it is who loves Me; and he who loves Me shall be loved by My Father, and I will love him, and will disclose Myself to him" (John 14:21). "If anyone loves Me, he will keep My word" (John 14:23). In Psalm 1, the role of the Word of God in transforming our lives is clear: "How blessed is the man who does not walk in the counsel of the wicked, nor stand in the path of sinners, nor sit in the seat of scoffers." The word "blessed" means "inwardly and spiritually satisfied," and Christ used the Greek form of the word in the Beatitudes to describe those living for the kingdom of heaven. It is the idea of experiencing inward, spiritual satisfaction, and it comes from spending time in God's Word

Verse 2 of Psalm 1 says, "But his delight is in the law of the LORD, and in His law he meditates day and night." The law of God has to do with the will of God. It is that which God orders and commands. The person is fully satisfied who comes to the Word seeking that which God wants him to do. The promises are all there. They are like the icing on the cake. But the whole attitude is, "Lord, I love You. I want to obey Your Word. I want to know Your will in my life. I'm submissive to Your will in my life." This is where the Word takes on a brand-new perspective in our walk.

God's Love Letter

The Bible is like a love letter from God to His children. I don't know a lot about love letters, but I remember writing a heartfelt letter one time. You see, when I was growing up, my daddy was my hero. No boy ever had a better dad than I had. He didn't say a lot, but he always let me know he loved me. Some of my best memories are growing up fly fishing with my father—just the two of us sitting quietly in a boat together. When I grew up and went off to college, it was the hardest thing I had ever done in my life. My mom slobbered all over me, but my dad just shook my hand and smiled. I wanted to grab him and give him a bear hug, but I was afraid I'd start bawling like a baby, so I simply shook his hand and tried to act brave. I was independent Wayne Barber, heading off on a 26-hour train ride from Roanoke, Virginia, to Clinton, Mississippi, and I thought I was ready to be on my own.

I called home 17 times my first month away. I used to call, weeping in loneliness, and it was always my dad who answered the phone. I could never tell him what I was going through, so I'd start chatting about the weather and the football team and anything else that made me sound mature and independent. But one rainy January afternoon, after I had flunked a test and felt at my absolute lowest, I couldn't get hold of him. Nobody answered the phone. I missed my dad something fierce, and I wanted to hug him and be with him that day, so I took out a pencil and paper and wrote him a letter.

It took forever to write the first words on the page. I finally screwed up my courage and wrote, "Dear Dad, I love you and I miss you so much." Once those words were out, the rest of it flowed. I told him how I felt about him, how important he was to me, and how much I admired him. It was a love letter, I guess, and I'd never written anything like it before. My mom even called me a week later to tell me how much it meant to him. Dad and I never really talked about the letter, but I was glad I'd written it.

About five years later, I was staying with my parents when my father suffered a massive heart attack. Since I was the oldest child, I had to take care of all the official papers and go to his office to pick up his personal effects. In my daddy's locker, where he worked at the *Roanoke Times and World News*, I found his Bible. When I opened it, a letter fell out. It was the letter I had sent him from college. The other men in the locker room said they had seen him reading it countless times, though they never knew what it was. The guys from his Bible study group told me he used to read it after reading his Bible every morning— a reminder that his son loved and appreciated him. I'm eternally grateful for that rainy afternoon in Clinton, Mississippi, when I decided I had to tell my dad how I felt.

In the same way, God has given us a letter, detailing His love and concern for us all. And we in turn have the opportunity to *be* letters. Every time we say yes to His will, we let Him know we love Him and are grateful for what He has done on our behalf. Obedience is our love letter back to God for sharing His Word with us. If expressing my love to my earthly father meant so much, imagine what it means to our heavenly Father when we do the same. When we let His Word transform our lives, we develop an entirely new attitude in life.

The book of Titus records the apostle Paul's instructions to Titus, whom Paul had left on the island of Crete to correct some problems among the believers there. The situation was a lot like what was going on in Corinth and Ephesus at that time. There was much wickedness.

There were over a hundred cities on the island of Crete, and Paul wanted Titus to appoint elders in each of those cities. Those elders were to be men who were capable of teaching the Word of God. Their character had to be there, but they had to have sound doctrine as well. It is doctrine that holds us straight up. This is what takes an upside-down world and turns it right side up.

The Word of God is a channel for loving God. If you want to love Him, then you want to know what He says. When you *know* what He says, you want to *do* what He says. You do that in the energy and power of the Spirit of God, tapping into the light that God now offers to you being transformed from within. This is how the Christ life begins to grow.

A New Perspective on Life

I have a good friend who has served the Lord faithfully as an evangelist for years. Like anyone in life, but especially for those on the front lines of evangelistic work, he has been through his share of trials and tribulations. On one occasion, while visiting Stone Mountain, Georgia, the Lord showed him the reality of how we are perfected in the spiritual life. But you have to understand Stone Mountain first.

Just outside Atlanta, Georgia, Stone Mountain is just that—a granite outcropping that rises about 700 feet above the surrounding area. On its north face are carved, in exquisite detail, three gigantic representations of the leaders of the Confederacy: Jefferson Davis and Generals Robert E. Lee and Stonewall Jackson, all on horseback. The sculpture was commissioned by the State of Georgia in 1917, and finally dedicated in 1970. It is an awe-inspiring work, overwhelming in its size and detail.

As my friend sat in the restaurant at Stone Mountain Park contemplating the sculpture before him—its size physically, the size of the vision it took to conceive it (it was to have had many more figures than three, but they were never completed), and the patience and perseverance required to complete it—it dawned on him that completing a sculpture like the Confederate memorial was a process of taking from the mountain, not adding to it. That is, the mountain was smaller after the completion of the sculpture than at its beginning, but far more beautiful and meaningful. All that had been required was a half-century of painstaking chipping and chiseling—the removal of every ounce of granite that was obscuring the images of the three leaders and their horses.

Suddenly my friend's spiritual eyes were opened. *Stone Mountain was a picture of the Christian life.* We begin life large in pride, large in ego, and large in ambition—big in the eyes of the world. To our largeness we expect God to add His beautifying graces, making us larger still. But then we become angry when we discover that God does not plan to bless our flesh. Instead, He begins to chip away at it. If we live the Christ life, we end life perhaps smaller in the eyes of the world, but with far more beauty and grace and meaning as a result of the Sculptor's hand. All through our life God is chipping away to reveal the image of Christ that is obscured by our granite-like will. We discover that, like the granite mountain, we must reflect the attitude of John the Baptist, who understood, even in the infancy of the kingdom, that he must decrease so that Christ could increase (John 3:30).

Transformation Takes Time

Like the tools that the sculptor, Gutzon Borglum, used—hammer, chisel, explosives, even a flame-thrower—to shape and smooth the granite, so God has tools that He uses to chip away our hard and rough exteriors to reveal Christ in us. And chief among His tools are trials. When we come up against a difficult situation of whatever sort—sickness, finances, relationships—we know that God is using it to transform us into what He wants us to be.

That is the clear message of Romans 8:28,29: "And we know that God causes all things to work together for good to those who love God, to those who are called according to His purpose. For whom He foreknew He also predestined to become conformed to the image of His son, that He might be the firstborn among many brethren." Of course, we don't like it. And if a mountain could speak, I dare say Stone Mountain would say it didn't like being picked at for half a century either. But I also suspect that for the years since, and the years ahead, it would confess to rather relishing the pleasure it brings to those who gaze upon it.

Do you see the point? Transformation takes time. How many nights must Borglum have looked back at the mountain, unable to discern any difference he had made in a single day. It was his knowledge that by a million swings of the hammer is a mountain transformed, and that each day, whether he could see it from a distance or not, the image had indeed begun to appear. Did not the writer to the Hebrews tell us the same thing? "All discipline for the moment seems not to be joyful, but sorrowful; yet to those who have been trained by it, afterwards it yields the peaceful fruit of righteousness" (Hebrews 12:11). That's a new perspective. We've never had it before. Only grace can open our eyes to see what God is doing.

We talked in an earlier chapter of how the fog lifts when you start surrendering to Christ and start obeying Him and walking by faith. You begin to see by a new set of eyes. Paul prayed for the Ephesians that "the eyes of your heart may be enlightened" (Ephesians 1:18). When you yield to Christ, God gives you a spiritual discernment and a "knowing" that you didn't have before.

But what does it mean to really "know"? There are two words for "knowing" in the Greek New Testament. One word is *ginosko* and the other is *eido*. Many Christians are familiar with the word *ginosko*, since it simply means "knowing or understanding facts," and was used to describe the "Gnostics" a heretical first-century sect. The word *eido* has been translated as "know" so many times that the true meaning of the word has been lost. It comes from the word *horao*, which means "to have a deep sense of understanding." It is not something you learn in school, but something you learn over time. When you are willing to surrender to Christ, God gives you perception and understanding you didn't have before.

The first thing you begin to realize when living the Christ life is that life does not work against you anymore. Life works *for* you. That's the beautiful opportunity of walking by grace. When you are committed to Christ and obeying His Word, you realize that He is orchestrating your life as you live it. This is found clearly in James 1:2: "Consider it all joy, my brethren, when you encounter various trials." If you weren't familiar with that verse already, you might think I was talking about a sadistic individual. Who wants to jump up and shout every time he has a trial? James must be saying more than meets the eye when you first read that verse.

The word "consider" means "calculate this and put it into your equation." To "consider it all joy" is a measured event, not an ongoing process. You reflect on your life and trials. You do this before the trial, you do it during the trial, and you do it after the trial because you know that God is in charge of your life and everything going on around you. The priority of thinking when it comes to the circumstances of life is to understand that God is in control. "Consider it all joy when you encounter various trials."

Tests and Trials

When I was reading this verse one day, it dawned on me that James didn't say *if* you encounter various trials but *when* you encounter various trials. The perspective we should have is that life is like a quarry. God is conforming us as Romans 8:28,29 says. The interesting thing is that He uses trials, difficulties, troubles, and the storms of life to conform us. We don't get to choose the tools that God uses to chip off all the rough edges of our life.

So many people think that when bad things happen it must be the devil attacking. It may be, but never forget that the devil is on a leash. He can do nothing unless God allows him to do it. In fact, Paul says that a messenger came from Satan to buffet him in the flesh to keep him from exalting himself. We know that Satan would have wanted Paul to exalt himself, so if the purpose of his attacks on Paul was to keep the apostle from exalting himself, then God must have ultimately been behind it.

Satan goes no further than the purpose that God prescribes. If Satan is working against us, God is even in control of that in allowing it to work for good in our life. A Christian should never say, "I'm doing okay, I guess, under the circumstances." You may be under some circumstances, but those circumstances are under the oversight of God! James says, "Consider it all joy, my brethren, when you encounter various trials." Maybe you have just come out of a trial, but never fear—more will come! That's the way life is.

Are you experiencing a trial? Welcome to the Christian life. God is using these trials to conform us into the image of Christ Jesus. These trials are our friends because they drive us to the end of ourselves.

An author friend of mine calls trials the "strange ministers of God." God uses trials to minister to us. We have a brand-new perspective when we encounter various trials. The Greek word for encounter has the idea of falling into something. You are into these trials before you even get a chance to think about them. The book of James is not a book about *works* but about *faith,* and when faith is real it works. If our faith is real, then we will be okay. We've already done the homework. If we are surrendered to Christ when the trial comes, we will be ready to remain surrendered throughout the trial.

Here's what usually happens: Most of the time we stumble into the trial, and it is like a pop quiz. Remember how it was in school? You walk into the classroom and the teacher says, "Take all your books off your desk and get out a clean sheet of paper." The purpose of this pop quiz is to test us. The teacher has been telling us every day to study, and we said we would. He wants to find out if we have in fact been studying, so he tests us. That is the exact nature of trials in the spiritual life—to see if we are in fact being trained as we go along.

Listen to how Moses put it to the Israelites in Exodus 20:20: "Do not be afraid; for God has come in order to test you, and in order that the fear of Him may remain with you, so that you may not sin." Trials are like God's pop quizzes for life. You can tell people you have faith and that you love Jesus, and at some point God will say, "Okay, let's find out." So He puts a test into your life.

Everybody has some sort of organizer notebook or calendar, right? Wouldn't it be wonderful to sit down with your planner on Monday and say, "Lord, I know I need a trial in my life. How about this Thursday afternoon at 4:00 P.M. No, make that 4:30. I have to get my hair cut at 4:00." On Thursday you get up early in the morning. You memorize all the Scripture you can. You quote the verses, claim the promises, pay up your tithe, and mail offerings to all your favorite ministries. You're covered with the blood, dressed in the armor, filled with the power, and singing the praises. When 4:30 arrives, you grit your teeth and meet that trial head-up. Swoosh—it's a slam dunk, and everything's back to normal. Instead of crawling down a rocky road, you're enjoying a big bowl of Rocky Road ice cream to celebrate. Now that's the way to go through a

trial, right? Poor Job—he should have been more organized.

Unfortunately, life doesn't work that way. God gives
us trials that come upon us before we recognize them.
They drive us to the end of ourselves. And that is the best
thing that can happen to us.

The Multicolored Grace of God

A man walked into our church one day and said, "Can
I talk to you?"

I'm not much of a counselor, but I said, "Well, I guess
so." I was the only one left in the building, so I didn't have
much of a choice. After he left, he probably wished he had
not found me. He told me the worst story I've ever heard
in my life. Had I not been a Christian I would have said,
"Why don't you just go out and shoot yourself?" But God
began to give me the wisdom that this man was in the perfect position to be helped. So I said to this man after he finished telling his story, "Do you realize that you are in the
best place you could possibly be?"

He looked at me and said, "Are you crazy? Have you
heard anything I've said?"

"Can you tell me now all the things that you can't do
to solve your situation?"

"All the things I can't do is why I'm here."

"Good, when you're at the place where you realize
what you *can't* do, you're at the point to realize what God
can do."

That's what trials do. They drive us to the end of ourselves. In Psalm 107 David talks about the man who is
trying to walk on a ship that is out at sea. He walks like a
drunken man who cannot stand up. He says the storm
drove him to his wit's end. As Major Ian Thomas put it, we
need to get to our wit's end because then we are ready to
say, "God, I can't." Then God can say back to us, "I know.

I never said you could, but I can, and I always said I would."

In the "various trials" of James 1:2, the word "various" literally means "multicolored." When I was working for the telephone company years ago, we had to learn color codes for connecting various phone wires. In fact, it was the people at the telephone company who suggested strongly that I go into the ministry after I knocked 8000 telephones out of service in one night when I was working as a cable-splicer's helper.

Here I was trying to splice a phone cable together in the middle of the night, up on a telephone pole, with the wind howling around me. Now the rules for splicing cables are simple: When you have something that is red you put it with something else that is red. If it is yellow, you put it with something else that is yellow. If it is a color, it goes with something else of that same color. Complicated, isn't it? Well, because some of the colors looked like other colors in the middle of the night in poor light, I proceeded to splice the wrong colors together. It took the phone company two days to get service restored to those 8000 phones. (That's when they suggested to me, "Wayne, we really think you are called into the ministry. We think that you would do God and our customers a favor if you would go into that work.") Just like those phone wires, the trials that God orchestrates in our life are color-coded. Let me explain what that means.

First Peter 4:10 says, "As each one has received a special gift, employ it in serving one another as good stewards of the manifold grace of God." "Manifold" is the same Greek word translated "various" in James 1:2. It is the multicolored grace of God, the transforming power of God. Have you ever thought about the fact that if I'm going through a red trial, God already has the red grace that is needed to go along with that trial? The exact grace and exact enablement and exact transforming power that

I need are already there. I need only turn to Him, surrender to Him, and appropriate that grace.

In Ephesians 3:10, as Paul is talking about the churches
and the mystery that God has unveiled to Paul, he uses
this same word: "In order that the *manifold* wisdom of God
might now be made known through the church to the
rulers and the authorities in the heavenly places." The
word "wisdom" has the idea of the practical use of truth. I
can know God's Word, but God has to give me the
wisdom to know how to apply it to my given situation. If
I'm going through a red trial, God not only gives me the
red grace which enables me to bear up under it and be
transformed because of it, but He even gives me the red
wisdom to walk through it.

The Christlike Perspective

It is not that we are put into these trials for no reason
at all. We can count it all joy because, as we live the Christ
life, we have a Christlike perspective. (Do you remember
Christ's perspective in the Garden of Gethsemane? "Not
my will, but Thine be done." We can make this our first
priority in life.) If a trial happens, God has a purpose in it.
That's why James says, "Consider it all joy, my brethren,
when you encounter various trials." The word for "trial"
normally was used when something was inadequate or
unworthy. For example, John used that word in John 6:6
when Jesus tested Philip. Jesus was trying to show the disciples their own inadequacy, how they did not measure up
when they tried to feed the multitudes. But He also
showed them His adequacy. That word is meaningful to
me when I remember that I am sinful. It serves as a
reminder to show me the inadequacies of my flesh.

Our flesh always wants to take the easy way out. It's
our nature. Whenever I get under a pressure situation in
my church, my first reaction is to resign. That is the easiest

way out. I've written a lot of resignation letters that I could sell for a lot of money because of the stories they tell. They burn everybody biblically, and they justify my position. Trials pull out that which is inadequate about me and expose my flesh.

James 1:3 says, "Knowing that the testing of your faith produces endurance." The word "testing" here it has to do with proving something that is worthy and genuine. We know that God always shows the inadequacy of the flesh, but if we will trust Him and let Him supply His multicolored grace and wisdom, He not only proves Himself to us but proves us to ourselves. We see who we really are in Christ. We see that when we are pushed to the end, we will turn to Him. That is the Spirit of God living in us.

The word "endurance" means "the ability to bear up under whatever comes our way." In verse 4 James says, "Let endurance have its perfect result, that you may be perfect and complete, lacking in nothing." The word perfect doesn't mean "perfect" in the sense that we usually think of it. It has more to do with the sense of completion, the accomplishment of a task or a goal. God has a purpose in each trial that comes about in our life. If we respond properly to each trial in our life, then God will give us the grace and the wisdom to walk through it, and that in itself will prove our faith is genuine. He has a purpose in trials. When we have fulfilled that purpose we will be complete and perfect in our faith, lacking in nothing.

In the midst of your trial, stop asking God to lift it off you. Stop asking for an easy way out. Say, "God, all I need is You. I am complete in You. All I need is for You to do whatever You need to do in my life through this trial." At that point you've just passed the test. Whether God leaves the trial in your life or takes it away is not the point. The point is your passing it. And passing comes when you submit to Him in the trial, not when the trial leaves.

When Tragedy Strikes

If you are not living a surrendered life, confessing sin, dying to self, and living under the authority of the Word of God, you most likely do not have this perspective. In fact, you probably see yourself as a victim of at best a weak God and at worst an uncaring one. That's how the world accuses God whenever a "trial" happens to humanity: "If there is a God, He is either powerless or hateful or both. If He has power, why doesn't He remove the trial? If He has love, why would He have allowed it in the first place? He must have neither, and therefore He is not worthy of our belief."

I trust our discussion so far has already answered those objections. God is not in the business of making our lives all sweetness and light. He is in the business of chipping away our exteriors so that the image of Christ can emerge. The most painful thing He could take us through is motivated by His love and orchestrated by His power. Under God's authority and by God's grace, you are no longer a victim. Instead, God is using the trial to form you into the image of Christ Jesus. It is imperative that you understand this. But you won't understand it until you start living under the grace principle of a surrendered life.

When God opens your eyes, you will see life from His perspective. You won't panic. You won't run. Even when the temptation is there, God will prove you genuine in the midst of that situation. He will chip off a lot of you in order to conform you into the image of Christ Jesus.

A lot of people say, "I like what you just shared about James. That helps me when my boss comes in and he's cranky or when my car won't start, but what about when real tragedy strikes? What about when I'm at the point where I don't even know how to pray?" This happens to all of us. We may have a traumatic experience that we can't possibly begin to understand. We wonder what in the world is going on. We move from the realm of a trial to the realm of genuine suffering as a result of the trial. Is there something in Scripture that can lift me above those very sad, difficult, and tragic times?

The whole context of Romans 8 addresses these times in our lives. It is about the ministry of the Holy Spirit. You have to fit chapter 8 into the context of chapters 6 (our death to sin and identification with Christ) and 7 (trying to live life in our own strength). In chapter 8 we learn that the Holy Spirit gives us the power to do what we cannot do ourselves. Romans 8:25 says, "But if we hope for what we do not see, with perseverance we wait eagerly for it." We know that Christ is coming to get His church. We know that we are going to have a glorified body. The Christian knows where he is headed.

But look what he says in verse 26: "And in the same way the Spirit also helps our weakness; for we do not know how to pray as we should, but the Spirit Himself intercedes for us with groanings too deep for words." "Helps our weakness" is an as Aramaic word that expresses the intimacy of being together with someone, a camaraderie that cannot be separated. It is when someone comes and shares in something with another person. When you are in the midst of a dark trial, it is like you have been given a huge log to carry. You can barely pick up one end of it, much less the whole thing. In the midst of your wrestling with the burden, the Holy Spirit comes and picks up the other end of the log. He helps you with your weakness.

Our Loss and His Answers

What is our weakness in these situations? Sometimes it is being at a loss for words, not having the ability even to pray intelligently about the situation. When we are in these situations, it reflects one side of a two-sided coin of truth: 1) There is a God, and 2) you are not Him. The fact that we are not God, that we don't have the words, the answers, and the solutions, is exactly why we need Him. It is then that the Holy Spirit comes to pick up the other end of the log by interceding according to the will of God for us.

The Spirit intercedes for us with groanings too deep for words. You can't say them or hear them. When our little baby died at birth, and Diana and I had to work our way through that difficult situation, we didn't know this Scripture. If we had known it, we would have been able to know and rest in the fact that there was intelligible prayer being prayed, even if we weren't the ones who were praying. The Spirit of God knows the mind of God, and His will is good and acceptable and perfect.

We can also turn to 1 Thessalonians 5:18: "In everything give thanks; for this is God's will for you in Christ Jesus." We can trust that God is always in control. It is easy to read these words in a book or on the page of your Bible, but we have been through times since the death of our baby that were difficult, and we have found that these Scriptures are not just words on paper. They are life! When you are down so low that there's nowhere to look but up, then you will know that God the Holy Spirit is interceding for you. Not only will you thank Him for that, but you will thank Him for the situation that allowed you to realize that truth.

The believer has two advocates. Jesus not only intercedes for us constantly (1 John 2:1), but the Holy Spirit living in us picks up the other end of the log. When we can't pray, He is praying. Therefore, if my little child dies, that's the will of God for me. The Holy Spirit is praying the will of God. He knows the mind of God when I don't. If I don't get healed from my sickness, then I know that is the will of God. Whatever the circumstance or the result of my time of testing or suffering, I can trust God implicitly that He has done His will.

Romans 8:27, 28 says, "He who searches the hearts knows what the mind of the Spirit is, because He intercedes for the saints according to the will of God. And we know that God causes all things to work together for good to those who love God, to those who are called according to His purpose." Make sure you understand that the words "love God" are in the present tense. It is referring to those who are continuing to love God. What does Jesus say? "If you love Me, you will keep My word." If you're not going to stand on His Word, then you're going to have difficulty thinking you are "called according to His purpose" when trials and suffering come.

You may say, "I prayed for my daughter to live, but she died. How can that be good?" Good is not defined by us, but by God. Romans 8:29 says, "For whom He foreknew, He also predestined to become conformed to the image of His Son." What is the good that God is accomplishing in all the situations we encounter in life? It is to conform us to the image of Christ Jesus. Becoming like Christ, being conformed into the image of God's Son, is the greatest good.

Are you feeling a little like Stone Mountain, with parts of your exterior and interior flying in every direction as the Sculptor accomplishes His purpose? Just remember the words of one sculptor who was asked how he was able to sculpt a beautiful statue of a horse out of an ugly block of granite: "I just chip away everything that doesn't look like a horse."

God is chipping away from our lives everything that doesn't look like Christ. If you will stand on that truth, then Christ will be revealed in you in greater degrees every day. You may not notice the changes as much as you feel the pain. But from God's eternal perspective, He already is seeing you as conformed to the image of His Son.

A New Goal
in Ministry

This is a scary thought, but what if you and I had the ability to see into the hearts of people we associate with—to see their true motives? When someone did something nice for us, we would see the real reason. When someone asked us to do something for him or her, we would see his true motivation for asking. Like I said, it's a scary thought, made all the more scary by the fact that my own heart would be on display as well. I know what goes on in it, and sometimes it's not a pretty sight.

Before we get too far in our discussion, we need to remind ourselves that there is One who knows the heart of man (Genesis 20:6; Psalm 44:21), and there are times when God shows one person what is in another's heart (Acts 5:3-9—in this particular case, the persons with the dark hearts died, but the church gained a healthy fear of how serious God is about pure hearts). This leads me to the topic of this chapter.

There are many people in the church who, when they do something spiritual, are doing it for a selfish reason. In the crassest sense, they may stand to gain some personal benefit from it, as in the case of Ananias and Sapphira holding back part of the money they were professing to

133

give to the church. In a more subtle way, sometimes our motives are tainted by simply wanting to have a new experience of Christ. Almost like spinning a roulette wheel, we want to see what kind of result will come from the investment of our spiritual energy. Either way, we are doing it for ourselves, not for the glory of Christ.

When we become serious and aware of the Christ life, when we start experiencing what Paul prayed for the Ephesians in chapter 3—being strengthened in the inner man and comprehending the love of God—then we begin to be filled with the fullness of God. The next thing that happens in our lives is the reorienting of our motives. No longer are we serving Christ to receive something for ourselves, but we are serving Christ out of an attitude that wants Christ to receive glory. That is the bottom-line motivation we must have if we are living the Christ life—to allow Him to be glorified so that He might be recognized.

The word for glory, *doxa*, means "to give recognition to." That is the ultimate purpose of our time on this earth, that the world might see Christ in us. Wherever we go we take Him to a needy world. But if the glory is on us, then no one sees Him. Think of having a small, exquisite, original oil painting, just a few inches square. If that priceless object is placed in an ornate, gilded, two-foot-square frame, what do you think people will see first when they enter the room? If people are seeing us more than they are seeing Christ, then something is out of balance.

That Christ would be glorified is part of Paul's prayer in Ephesians 3:20,21. He writes, "Now to Him who is able to do exceeding abundantly beyond all that we ask or think, according to the power that works within us, to Him be the glory in the church and in Christ Jesus to all generations forever and ever. Amen." The members of the body of Christ are to let the Lord be recognized in them. Whatever we do, we let Him be in charge of us and be jseen in us, so that no glory would come to us, our church, or our denomination.

Paul then says in Ephesians 4:1, "I, therefore, the prisoner of the Lord, entreat you to walk in a manner worthy of the calling with which you have been called." We have to learn to let Christ be recognized in us. When Paul "entreats" us, it means he is asking us, reminding us, almost pleading with us, to let our lives reflect our calling. Our calling was a holy calling (2 Timothy 1:9), and our lives must be holy as well in order that Christ be glorified.

Who Gets the Glory?

I can remember back before God broke through to me about this truth. I am ashamed to say, looking back, that almost everything I did, even in ministry, was for some sort of selfish gain. If I was running a basketball tournament, I wanted the glory for running a good tournament. If it was a camp that I was directing, I wanted the honorarium so we could buy a new piece of furniture. Whatever I was doing, I had figured out a way for it to benefit me—until God broke me of that and showed me that everything should benefit Him. I'm supposed to live so that all credit and all glory goes to Him—and He will meet my needs exceeding abundantly beyond all that I could ask or think. That was a radical change in my life, one that did not come easily. But I began to realize that whatever I did, I had to make sure that all the glory went to Him.

When you walk in a manner worthy of the Lord, the idea of "worthy" is a set of scales, and on each side is an equal weight. The weight that is on one side of the scales is clarified in Ephesians chapters 1, 2, and 3. It is all that we have in Christ, how to appropriate that, and how to let Christ be who He is in us. We sing a song in our church, "Jesus, be Jesus in me, no longer me but Thee. Resurrection power, fill me this hour, Jesus, be Jesus in me." That is one side of the balance. The other side is *living it out,* which is what Paul covers in chapters 4, 5, and 6. If you are going to tell people you believe chapters 1, 2, and 3 of Ephesians, then you are also going to have to live those chapters. That's what it means to live worthy—to balance what we say and do, to make sure our walk matches our talk.

Paul begins illustrating the evidence of chapters 1-3 right at the beginning of Ephesians 4: ". . .with all humility and gentleness, with patience, showing forbearance to one another in love" (verse 2). Whenever these characteristics are seen in the church, God is being glorified. When you have people who are being humble, that is an attitude they have in themselves. They don't want anybody to see them. They only want people to see Christ. The word "gentleness" is really the word for brokenness. A person who is genuine has come to that place where he is strong, but his strength is under control. The word for patience is not referring to patience with our circumstances but patience with people—being willing to be longsuffering with people. Think about what the church would be like if we lived this way, walking worthy of our calling.

Next he says, "showing forbearance in love." The word "forbearance" has many nuances. One of the most beautiful to me is this: If I have a difference with one of my brothers in Christ, I so let Christ empower me that I will stand next to that brother and hold him up even though we have differences. I don't kick him out. I don't throw him away. I forbear with him until we are able to see our way through the disagreement or difficulty. Because men in their own strength cannot live this way, Christ gets the glory.

Paul goes on to say in verse 3, ". . . being diligent to preserve the unity of the Spirit in the bond of peace." If the church is going to bring glory to Christ, we are going to have to learn how to preserve the unity of the Spirit in the bond of peace. He doesn't say *produce* the unity; he says *preserve* the unity. We already have the unity in the Spirit. Christ is glorified when people see unity in the body of Christ, when every person is a minister, a servant, or a vessel through which He is working. When that happens, and people are walking in a worthy manner, then they are going to experience the unity that they already have.

You may look at your church and say, "Wayne, we don't have unity." Yes, you do in Christ. But if this unity in Christ is not evident, then someone is not walking in surrender to Christ. How do you preserve unity? In the bonds of peace. Peace means "no conflict." Remember, you have to lay your sword down. If I am not going to fight God, then I am not going to fight you either. I am going to let Christ in me love you through me. I am going to let my strength with which I could overpower you be under His control so that He can use me as a tender vessel for His glory.

Learning to Glory in Jesus

The glory of Christ becomes a brand-new goal in life. If He is glorified in everything in my life, and in every other person's life, then He will be glorified in my church. The only way He is going to be recognized in the church is through the spiritual unity into which He draws people together. This is not spiritual *conformity* we are talking about—everyone acting the same. We are talking about spiritual *unity.* We can be diverse—the church is that way. But we can have unity with diversity. When Jesus is in control of my life and yours, He will unite us and be seen in us.

That is Paul's message. That is our new goal. Whatever we do, we let Christ be recognized. In Ephesians 4:22 Paul talks about taking off the old self like taking off a garment. A garment is what people see on the outside, but we are dressed first on the inside. This garment of the old self can only come off when we have put on Christ Jesus. Paul is not talking about the old man, but about the *lifestyle you lived* in the old man. He says, "In reference to your *former manner of life* you lay aside the old self, which is being corrupted in accordance with the lusts of deceit, and . . .be renewed in the spirit of your mind" (Ephesians 4:22).

In Colossians 3:9-11 Paul says we already have laid aside the old self. Since we have done that, we should quit living as though we haven't. In other words, come back to living the victory that is yours. Let Christ be who He is in your life. He says in Ephesians 4:22, "Lay aside the old self, which is being corrupted in accordance with the lusts of deceit." There is a corruption to flesh life. It doesn't get better—it gets worse. So he says, "Come back to living the lifestyle that God has given to you."

Then he adds in verse 23 "That you be *renewed* in the spirit of your mind." That's where it all starts. We have to *think* differently and put on the new self. Again, we have already put on Christ, but now we need to let Him be seen in our life. Paul says in verse 24, "Put on the new self, which in the likeness of God has been created in righteousness and holiness of the truth." Now this is going to give evidence to the fact that you are living a surrendered life. When you glorify Christ and He is seen in and through you, your behavior will radically change. Remember, this is not a self-help program. This is not where you grit your teeth and say, "I'm going to do better." Flesh doesn't get better. But when you come and say, "I can't do better," and you are willing to die to your own will and your own agenda and you are willing to surrender yourself to Christ, then your behavior will be markedly different.

What we are talking about is the chief difference between religion and relationship. All religion is from the outside in. But Christianity is an *internal relationship with Christ*, so that the garment on the outside is affected by

His power, not your fleshly energy. Paul begins to show you what the difference is. In Ephesians 4:25 he says, "Therefore, laying aside falsehood, speak truth, each one of you, with his neighbor, for we are members of one another." This new garment will be a truthful garment. The first piece of armor that he tells you to put on in Ephesians 6 is the belt of truth. This does not refer to the Word of God. In Ephesians 6 the Word of God is referenced by the sword of the Spirit. Paul is simply talking about the need for truthfulness and honesty.

Jesus never lied, and therefore we shouldn't lie if Jesus is living in us. There can be no deception in our lives if Christ is being glorified. We can't be acting one way and then living another. What we speak is evidence of what we are. Paul says, "Speak truth to one another." If I am living a surrendered life, God's Spirit will not let me be deceitful in any way by what I say. Obviously that will transfer itself to what I do. I cannot be a deceitful person in my words or in my lifestyle. Being transparent and honest allows people to see Christ who lives in me.

Don't Give the Devil Opportunity

We once had a very convicting experience and learned an embarrassing lesson regarding speaking the truth in all things. My wife and I were eating lunch with our four-year-old daughter Stephanie one day when the phone rang. The call was for me, and my wife put her hand over the receiver and asked me, "Are you home?"

"No, no, no, tell them I'm gone."

"I'm sorry," my wife replied into the receiver, "he's not here right now, but he'll be at the church in about 45 minutes if you would like to talk to him."

I always tried to avoid calls when I had a few minutes to be at home with my family, so I really didn't think about what I had said. I finished my lunch and went back to the church. About 30 minutes later my wife called on the phone and said, "Repent! I'm telling you, you need to repent!"

"What do you mean, repent? For what? What did I do?"

"When you left, Stephanie looked up at me and said, 'Mom, is what you just did on the phone a lie?'"

My wife was caught suddenly with having to be honest and truthful. What was she going to say? "Well, Stephanie, I've been a Christian for several years and God lets older people lie. You can be deceitful. You can go to church and play games." Instead she said, "Yes, Stephanie, that's a lie."

Stephanie said, "Well, mom, if that's a lie, isn't that a sin?"

"Well, Stephanie, yes, that was a sin."

"Didn't you tell me that if I ever sinned I needed to confess that sin and ask God to forgive me?"

"Yes, I did."

"Well, come on." She took my wife's hand and led her back to the bedroom. They got down on their knees, and Diana confessed her sin of untruthfulness. Then she called me and told me to repent since I was the one who told her to tell the lie. And I did repent. Out of the mouths of babes comes understanding! I realized that in my jaded, adult world I had let the lines blur between believing the truth and living the truth. But in the innocent mind of a child, there was a huge inconsistency between our words and our actions.

We can't live that way. There can be no deceit in our lives. How much deceit is there in the church today? How often does our flesh manipulate people into thinking we are one thing when we know we're not? We can't live that way anymore. When we're living for Christ there can be no "me" in the picture. A deceitful lifestyle will stand out like a sore thumb if we're trying to manufacture an honest lifestyle.

Whose Anger?

Paul says in Ephesians 4:26, "Be angry, and yet do not sin; do not let the sun go down on your anger." That is an interesting phrase, "Be angry." My flesh likes that part, but it doesn't like the part that says, "Do not sin with the anger." What does that mean? Are there two kinds of anger? I read a book one time that said that all kinds of anger are sin. That is interesting because James 1:20 says, "The anger of man does not achieve the righteousness of God."

Now if there is an anger of man, could there be the anger of God? Obviously there is, for we see the anger of God all through Scripture. He is angry at sin, but He is a righteous God. His anger is a righteous anger. There is a fine line between righteous anger and worldly anger. Paul says, "Do not let the sun go down on your anger." That last word for anger means a "provoked anger." Never let the sun go down on provoked anger because it will bring bitterness. Bitterness will grow a root and defile many (Hebrews 12:15). How can I be angry and not sin with my anger?

Man's anger always has a person as its target. I deer hunt, and I have a scope on my rifle that has crosshairs in the middle of it. When I release the power of my rifle, it is going to impact whatever is in those crosshairs. If a person is not righteously angry, he has in his crosshairs an individual. And if he keeps that person in the crosshairs of his anger then the full force of his anger is going to eventually harm that person. But if a person is righteously angry, enabled by God's Spirit, then we never have a person in focus; we have the *problem* in focus. There is a big difference. God hated sin, but He so loved the world that He sent His son to die for the sinner that committed it. We love sinners, but we hate sin.

In my local area I am an advocate for the pro-life move-ment. Many people in my church are also involved in pro-life activities. We do a lot for pro-life issues because God is pro-life. There are people in our area who stand for the same cause that I stand for; however, some of the most antagonistic letters I have received over the years have been from them. These are people who have been linked to the same cause but who have a different perspective on methodology. They are *attacking people* rather than *addressing the problem*. When you have the garment of Christ on, you will never have people in your crosshairs, but will only have issues. Your anger will be a righteous anger.

By the way, if you are wondering whether your anger is righteous or unrighteous, go on and confess it as unrighteous. Chances are that you've not even experi-enced God's anger yet. God hates sin but weeps over sin-ners. There is a very delicate balance. If we have put on Christ's new garment, we will not have a vindictive spirit.

Ephesians 4:27 gives us a principle: "Do not give the devil an opportunity." Without the context of chapter 4, you could take that admonition and make it say whatever you want. A lot of people say the word "opportunity" is the word for "place," and it is used that way most of the time in the New Testament. However, it does not always mean "place." It can mean "opportunity," as when Paul was before Agrippa (Acts 25). Agrippa said, "We never sentence a man without giving him an opportunity to speak for himself." It is the same word, here plainly used to mean "opportunity."

By the way, this verse should not be used to say that a Christian can have a demon within him. The context of the passage is the unity of believers, which brings glory to Christ within the church. The word "devil" is *diabolos*—*dia* means "through" and *ballo* means "to cast." Put the words together and they mean "to cast in between and divide," which is Satan's favorite activity. If you are not going to

wear the right garment and bring Christ glory through
your life, you become a tool that the devil can use—an
opportunity or instrument for division. He doesn't even
have to be around. You have aligned yourself with his
system already if you are disrupting the unity of the body.
You are a divider of God's body.

A Life Changed by Christ

Ephesians 4:28 says, "Let him who steals steal no
longer, but rather let him labor, performing with his own
hands what is good, in order that he may have something
to share with him who has need." A person who steals is a
taker. He is taking what does not belong to him. But if you
have the right garment on, you are never a taker; you are
always a giver. And when you have the right garment on,
you don't give so that you can get something back. You
give because that is what Christ is motivating you to do
with your life.

You are a replenisher, not a depleter. Depleters will
drain everything out of you. They are like parasites who
don't care about anything except what they can get from
you; and after you they move on to someone else. Unfortunately, there are parasites in the church who claim to be
believers but are wearing the wrong garment. When you
have the right garment on, you are a giver of time, talent,
and treasure—not a depleter. You are always giving to the
needs that you see around you. In reality, it is not *you*
giving, but Christ in you. That brings glory, identification,
and recognition to Him.

Ephesians 4:29 says, "Let no unwholesome word pro-
ceed from your mouth, but only such a word as is good for
edification according to the need of the moment, that it
may give grace to those who hear." Two key words in this
verse—one negative, one positive—provide the paradigms for speech in the Christ life. The first word is

unwholesome. The word "unwholesome" is actually the word for "rotten"—something that is very smelly. It is the smell of my son's tennis shoes that he puts in the garage—which I've told him can make the car back out by itself.

Try maintaining peace and unity in the body the next time someone begins to share an unwholesome word or a piece of gossip with you. Just say, "Something smells terrible around here. You'll have to excuse me; I've got to get away from this smell." You would stop that gossip from going any farther.

The word for edification, however, is the word which means "to build a house." It doesn't mean you don't say things that are hard or difficult; it means that you say them in such a way that it builds a person up and does not tear him or her down.

In high school, my football coach would always tell me to make sure I ran my pass pattern at least ten yards on a third-down pass in order to get the first down. I was big for my age, but coach was huge—6'8" and over 300 pounds (yes, he had played professional football). In a particular game we played, my pass pattern was called on the third down. I tried to run the pattern ten yards deep, but I was double-covered and couldn't get downfield. The quarterback threw the pass over my head, but I made a diving catch—without getting the first down. I was proud of my great catch as I trotted off the field.

My coach walked up to me on the sideline and very firmly and angrily picked me up off the ground and said to me, "Barber, when are you ever going to learn to run the pass pattern like I told you!" When he dropped me, I felt defeated. But then he turned around and said, "By the way, Wayne . . ."

I said, "Yes, sir?"

"Man, what a great catch!"

He told me what I needed to hear, but he didn't tear me down with it; he built me up. That's what the Spirit of

God wants to help us do—edify people, building them up in their lives and in their faith.

In Ephesians 4:30 Paul says, "And do not grieve the Holy Spirit of God, by whom you were sealed for the day of redemption." That is the fundamental principle in all of this. When you are grieving the Spirit, you are giving the devil an opportunity. Paul says, "Don't do it." The word "grieve" is a love word. If I live sensitive to His leadership, His authority in my life, letting His Word dominate me, I'm not going to *grieve* Him. I'm going to *please* Him. As a result, I'm going to maintain the unity of the Spirit and God will be glorified in my life and in the church.

In Ephesians 4:31,32 Paul says, "Let all bitterness and wrath and anger and clamor and slander be put away from you, along with all malice. And be kind to one another, tender-hearted, forgiving each other, just as God in Christ also has forgiven you." He takes the worst thing and works it back to its source. Malice is the essence of the old garment. Malice is the fabric of the flesh. Malice is that underlying desire that wants to see another person harmed. Paul works his way back through the way malice is expressed: bitterness, wrath (the explosiveness of the emotion), anger (the seething thing that is about to explode), clamor (the loud arguing), and slander (speaking against another person). All of this comes out of the rotten pit of malice. Malice is what we have been saved from and therefore not what we are supposed to be seen as.

Look at the astounding difference in the garment pictured in verse 32: "And be kind to one another, tender-hearted, forgiving each other, just as God in Christ also has forgiven you." When you wear that kind of garment, Christ is glorified and can be seen in you and through you. That's the new perspective that the Christ life brings.

I began this chapter suggesting how scary it would be if we could see into each other's hearts and know the actual motivations behind the actions. Let me end it by telling you something even more scary: The nature of the garment which is our outer man is an infallible indicator of the thoughts and intents of the heart. Is the outer man lined up with the Word of God? Then so is the inner man. Is the outer man lined up with the carnal behaviors of the flesh? Then be assured that the heart is centered in the flesh as well. You and I don't need to be able to see much deeper than today's words and actions in order to tell the condition of the heart. Is that scary enough for you?

A New Strength
for Warfare

Think of all the different instances of people preparing themselves for battle. Tour the museums and castles of the British Isles and Europe and you'll see suits of armor designed to protect medieval combatants. Even the horses were clothed with coats of mail, or armor mesh. By the time of the American Revolution, and later the Civil War, cannon and muskets allowed long-distance contact, so armor fell out of use. And in today's science fiction thrillers, weapons from the minds of futurists vaporize the enemy down to the last atom. If a Christian looks through books on the history of warfare and weaponry, it is impossible not to be struck with the contrast between the weapons used by the armies of men and the weapons used by the army of the Lord.

For instance, the one person who entered the single most threatening conflict in all of history did so clothed only in a simple robe. No gun, no shield, no bayonet, no laser, no X-ray vision. Jesus Christ engaged Satan, the prince of the power of the air, with no weapons other than truth, righteousness, and the Holy Spirit. Granted, the people of God sometimes used swords and spears to accomplish His purposes in the Old Testament. But Paul reminds us that the weapons of our warfare are not fleshly, but are divinely ordered (2 Corinthians 10:3-6). We are called to wage war today in exactly the same fashion as did Jesus—with divinely ordained means. In this chapter we look at the believer's spiritual armor.

In the last chapter we talked about the garment of Ephesians 4, with which we are clothed externally as a result of the submission of our wills to Jesus Christ. When we are empowered by Christ, that garment is our lifestyle. On sports teams, there is always an offense and a defense. There is a sense in which the garment of Ephesians 4 represents the offense of our battle. It is what we go about doing in the power of the Holy Spirit to extend the values of the kingdom of God wherever we go. We speak the truth, we do not become sinfully angry, we do not steal, we work for what we receive, we don't use unwholesome speech, we build up others in our conversation. All of these characteristics become the garment we wear just as they were for Jesus.

But when we come to Ephesians 6, Paul reminds us that we are in fact in a war. There is a spiritual enemy that seeks to hurt us, and we therefore must be prepared defensively to withstand the attack of the enemy. It becomes an eye-opener to most believers when they discover that the basis of their defense is the same as the basis of their offense—the Person of the Lord Jesus Christ, to whom we are submitted in the inner man. As we said in the last chapter, it is Christ in me that allows me to do good to others. And we will see in this chapter that it is Christ's righteousness that also protects me from the attack of the enemy. Did Satan ever bring permanent harm to Jesus Christ? Not once. And he will bring no permanent harm to the believer who remains in Christ. Let's look at the spiritual armor that God gives us in Christ.

The Warrior-Messiah

In Isaiah 59:17 there is a prophetic reference to the coming of Messiah. It says, "And He put on righteousness like a breastplate, and a helmet of salvation on His head; and He put on garments of vengeance for clothing, and wrapped Himself with zeal as a mantle." We worship a Warrior-Messiah. He is the One who conquered sin and who conquered Satan. He is the One who conquers my flesh and who rendered sin powerless in my life. He is the One who delivered me from the penalty of sin and will raise me and give me a glorified body. He is the One who has to be the garment and the armor.

Many people are writing books today about spiritual warfare. My caution is to be very careful—and very biblical—about what you read and embrace. It is a simple reality that we have thousands of years of military metaphors that fill our minds. Warfare is a significant part of human history. But this doesn't mean that it is appropriate to automatically transfer all of those metaphors to the biblical references about spiritual warfare. Remember what Paul clearly said: *We do not war according to the flesh.* Nearly 100 percent of our knowledge about warfare comes from the realms of the flesh, so we must be careful not to construct paradigms for spiritual warfare out of our history books. We must remain simply, yet profoundly, biblical in this arena.

In Ephesians 6:10 Paul says, "Finally, be strong in the Lord, and in the strength of His might." The word "finally" does not mean that he is now teaching on a brand-new subject—a new topic called spiritual warfare. For the most part, the Scriptures are not collections of topical dissertations on various subjects. In the case of Ephesians, Paul is writing a brief but complete overview of the Christian life for the church at Ephesus. And here he begins summing up the book. He wants to tie together everything he has said and put it in a different perspective so that he might get our attention.

We have to ask: If spiritual warfare is the be-all and end-all of the Christian life, as some say it is, and if we should set this section apart and develop an entire category of spiritual discipline from it, then why did Paul take only ten verses to talk about it in the very last chapter of the letter to Ephesus? The reason is that he is wrapping up the letter, and reminding us of the source of the fleshly conflicts that he has been warning us about. We are in a war every day we live on planet Earth. It doesn't mean that Satan is going to personally come jump on me every day. But it does mean that the whole world is under the control of the evil one (1 John 5:19). The Son of God has come and has given us understanding (1 John 5:20). He has come to destroy the devil's work (1 John 3:8). The bottom line is that He who is in us is greater than he who is in the world (1 John 4:4).

Think of it this way: When the Allied Forces stormed the beaches of Normandy on D-Day, the fate of the Axis powers under Hitler was sealed. For all practical purposes, the war was over. There was no way the German forces could withstand such an onslaught. But it still required many months of fierce fighting for the victory to be sealed. In a similar way, *believers are going to encounter fierce opposition from Satan even though his fate was sealed by the death and resurrection of Christ.* Satan's ultimate weapon, death, was defeated when Christ walked out of the tomb (1 Corinthians 15:54-57). The battle has been fought and the victory won, but Satan is not going to go away without a fight. He will continue to fire salvos at the believer until his final banishment.

The surest way for the believer to remain protected is to keep his or her armor in place, which simply means remaining surrendered to Jesus Christ at all times. Believers love to quote James 4:7b, "Resist the devil and he will flee from you," while forgetting verse 7a: "Submit therefore to God." Does that make it plain enough about where our protection lies? And yet, as we said in the early chapters of this book, submitting to God is our choice. (Notice all the commands—our responsibility—that are given in connection with the spiritual armor.)

Ephesians 6:10 says, "Finally, be strong in the Lord and in the strength of His might." All three of these words for strength (strong, strength, and might) are unique and have been used earlier in this epistle. There are four words for strength found in Scripture, and three of them occur in this verse. First, Paul says, "Be strong." Be enabled with ability you don't have yourself. Then he says, ". . . in the strength," a word which literally means "proven strength" or "dominion."

When I was growing up, we used to play king of the mountain. If you could get up on the hill, all of your buddies would try to knock you off. If you could throw everyone off, you were king of the mountain. You had proven your skill and you got to have dominion over that mountain. That is the essence of the word Paul uses here.

Obviously, it is not our strength or dominion, but Christ's. It is almost laughable to think of humans having dominion over anything. And yet remember that Adam was indeed given dominion over everything (Genesis 1:28; 2:15). When Adam lost it, it was necessary for the last Adam to regain dominion (1 Corinthians 15:45). It is now in Christ alone that we can have any dominion at all. Stepping outside of the dominion and strength of Christ is a good way to attract the enemy, for he knows that on our own we are weak. The enemy defeated the first Adam in Eden, but failed to defeat the last Adam in the wilderness (Luke 4:1-13). By remaining in Christ we remain in the One who has won dominion over all things.

Impressed by His Presence

Look through the New Testament and just see what Christ can do. Do you realize that the power of His resurrection is the epitome of His power? Paul says, "I want to know the power of His resurrection" (see Philippians 3:10). We can tap into that power. He has proven Himself to be strong and to have dominion.

Then Paul says, "Be strong in the strength of His might." The word for might means "the inherent strength of somebody." Christ doesn't have to do anything to *gain* strength. Just as He said He is the way, the truth, and the life, so also is He the strength. He doesn't *get* strength; He *is* strength. Just sitting in His presence is enough for you. By being in Him we participate in His might.

My wife, children, and I were at an amusement park when a professional football player got on the same elevator we were on. I have never seen a bigger person. He was taller than I am (I'm 6'7"). His arms were bigger than my legs. The little child he was carrying looked like a little teddy bear he might have won throwing balls at a booth. It wasn't necessary for me to get on a football field to see what he could do. Just standing a few inches from him was all I needed to gauge his might. Being in his presence told me all I needed to know. If you think standing in the presence of a large human being is impressive, what do you think standing in the presence of the ascended Lord Jesus Christ would be like? (Read Revelation 1:10-17 to find out.)

In light of the strength of Christ, try to grasp this point as it relates to our relationship with Him: If we would daily practice the presence of Christ, invoking His strength, asking Him to enable us, and letting Him be the One who fills our mind with His will, we wouldn't have to see Him do anything because we would know what He can do simply by His presence. So often, we make the mistake of the Pharisees, who wanted Jesus to give them a sign. These supposed shepherds of Israel didn't have as much discernment as the sheep they were supposed to be leading, because the sheep recognized Jesus' authority simply by being in His presence and listening to His words (Matthew 7:28,29). When we begin to place more value on what Jesus *does* than on the simple truth of who He is, we may be getting out of balance.

Our Real Enemy

In Ephesians 6:12 Paul said, "For our struggle is not against flesh and blood, but against the rulers, against the powers, against the world forces of this darkness, against the spiritual forces of wickedness in the heavenly places." That ought to be put over every doorpost of every church. It should be on your mirror so that you will see it in the morning when you wake up. We do not fight against flesh and blood—even in the world, and especially in the church. Our brother is not our enemy. *Satan* is the enemy. We love lost humanity, and we pray for them to be released from the grasp of the enemy. If we have conflict in the body of Christ, we pray for our unity to be manifested. No unbeliever or believer is ultimately our enemy. The only flesh on this earth that can be a problem for me is my own.

Many books on spiritual warfare cite verse 12 as a hierarchy of satanic and demonic authority. That may well be, since we know that Satan tries to copy everything God does, and God is highly organized. But there is another side to this. The word "ruler" is the word *arche*. It means "the originator of something." Do you want to know where evil comes from in this world? The origination of all evil comes from Satan. We struggle against the originator of evil.

We also struggle against the powers of evil. The word translated "power" means "that which has the right and the might." In God's light Satan has *no* right or might. It is only in the darkness where right by might is exercised. Not surprisingly, Paul says that we battle against darkness, and "against the world forces of this darkness." We also battle against ". . . the spiritual forces of wickedness in the heavenly places." The picture is of the lower heavens being completely encompassed in darkness that came as a result of the fall of Adam. But the darkness is only temporary. We know this because anytime we see a word for Satan as a ruler it is the Greek word *krataios* (ruler), but when you see Jesus, it is *pontokrator* (ruler over all). Satan is limited to this world. God has authority over him and over all things.

If that is true, then nothing can penetrate Satan's darkness but light. And God is light. He is not *like* light; He *is* light. Nobody will ever turn Him on and nobody will ever turn Him off. He pierced that darkness and became light to all men (John 1:9). Now, Paul says in Ephesians, *we too have been made light.* We become the light to others. Darkness has never yet put out light. Instead light dispels darkness. The intense focus that many people have on the devil is the wrong focus. We need to focus on the *light*. The One who conquered the darkness, the One who lives in us, will conquer darkness in our life.

Taking Up God's Armor

In Ephesians 6:13 does Paul suggest, "Therefore, take up the full armor of God, and go everywhere in your city. Find the stronghold that Satan is over, and cast him down and bind him so that he will not bother any of the Christians"? Is that what he said? No. What he really said was, "Therefore, take up the full armor of God, that you may be able to resist in the evil day, and having done everything, to stand firm." He does not tell me to go after the devil. He doesn't tell me to do anything but to stand firm and resist him. How do I resist him? By submitting to God and clothing myself in the garment of Christ as I surrender to Him. *"Take up* the full armor of God."

Many believers make a practice of daily reading Ephesians 6 and "putting on" the armor of God in prayer. Personally, I used to get a little confused as to which piece I had just put on. Now I realize that I put on Christ. He is all of those pieces put into one, the "whole armor of God." Why do we put it on? Ephesians 6:13 says, "That you may be able to resist in the evil day, and having done everything, to stand firm." The word "resist" has the idea of standing up to someone face-to-face. There is no armor to protect your back. In other words, you don't run from Satan—ever. You walk right into his territory, and you walk into it armed with the garment of Jesus Christ.

Christ is your garment and your armor. He has already defeated Satan. A wimpy demon could whip all of us, but could not touch the Lord Jesus who lives in us. That is the key. He is our armor and our warrior. Paul tells us in verses 14 and 15 how to stand: "Stand firm therefore, having girded your loins with truth, and having put on the breastplate of righteousness, and having shod your feet with the preparation of the gospel of peace." The idea of standing firm is being immovable. The Greek word for loins has to do with the five lower vertebrae in the back.

Have you ever tried to stand up with a weak back? I bought a car one time because people said to be financially free you should buy a gas saver. I am 6'7" and I bought a gas saver which was made for people who are 5'2" or less. I was jammed in that little car thinking I was saving money and was going to get out of debt.

One day in the church parking lot I completely threw my back out when I was twisting to get myself out of that little matchbox. I could not even stand up. On all fours I crawled to the church and banged on the door. The secretary opened it and said, "Wayne, will you quit clowning? We've got work to do." They thought I was faking it because I was always kidding around. I lay there for 20 minutes or so until one of them finally realized I was really hurt. (In fact, to give the secretary credit, she is still apologizing to me today for not realizing I was really hurt.) I was on my back on the floor and could not do anything for two weeks. I could not even get in my bed. When your lower back is damaged, you can do little of anything.

The truth is like your back: It is the strength for everything else. And Paul says our loins need to be girded with truth, as opposed to deceit. The truth can be the gospel or it can be the way we live. It goes back to what we talked about earlier in the last chapter: Don't live a deceitful lifestyle. If you are going to wear the garment, and you are going to wear the armor, then make up your mind to do so.

The Rest of the Armor

The next piece of armor is "the breastplate of righteousness." The breastplate covers the chest area that includes your heart. What is righteousness? Righteousness is that which comes by faith in the Word of God through Christ. Righteousness is what He produces in us. With righteousness, it is not just the activity of what He does through you, but it is also the heart motivation for why you do it. It is having the willingness to serve Him and to walk by faith. Romans 1:17 says, "For in it the righteousness of God is revealed from faith to faith; as it is written, 'But the righteous man shall live by faith.'"

The first step is to make my decision not to be deceitful to anybody. I am going to put on the belt of truth. I am going to be an honest person in the way I approach everything. There is to be no lying in me. That leads to my heart motivation. I don't want to do works in my own flesh. I want God to produce His works in me. My heart is to be protected by that message of what righteousness is all about.

Then Paul says in Ephesians 6:15, "having shod your feet with the preparation of the gospel of peace." Roman soldiers wore sandals that had cleats on the bottom, like modern golf shoes. They would go into battle and dig in. This is important to understand because these cleats were something that would hold them up in warfare.

What is it that holds us steady and keeps us immovable? The good news of peace. The gospel gives us a firm foundation. First, a person must have peace with God, and second, peace with man. It is not just the fact that you were saved one day by the gospel, it goes beyond that. The gospel is not just for the lost; it's also for the saved. We need to have a firm grasp of what the message of grace is or else we won't be able to stand in the face of the enemy we must battle every day of our lives.

Verse 16 says, ". . . in addition to all, taking up the shield of faith, with which you will be able to extinguish all the flaming missiles of the evil one." The idea is that taking up the shield of faith is something you do daily. The first three things are principles of your life that cannot be moved. On the basis of those three immovable principles, take up the shield of faith.

There are two words for "shield" in biblical Greek. There is the small shield that a soldier would carry and also a door-sized shield. When armies were locked in combat they would fire flaming arrows at each other. Which shield would you rather have—the little shield or the door-sized shield? Personally, I want the door shield to hide behind when they launch the flaming arrows.

That is the word used here. These huge shields were rectangular in form with grooves on the sides. A line of soldiers, arm-in-arm, would have those shields hooked together like a long, rectangular wall. Behind the wall of shields would be the reinforcements. As soon as the flaming arrows hit those leather-covered shields they would be extinguished. If a soldier was hit, another would step up from behind and replace him. He would grab the shield and get in step with the advancing wall. When I have the willingness to do what God says I should do (and when the whole church locks their shields of faith together!), then the shield will be raised to protect me from evil attacks.

The word for the evil one is the word that means "intentionally out to harm you." The system of the world, as a reflection of its leader, is out to harm us. Satan wants to destroy us. That is what God has saved us from. That is why believers are a unique group. We, among all the peoples living in the world system, are sanctified and saved from the eternal effects (and many of the temporal effects) of that system. When we have our shield of faith in place, it extinguishes the missiles which the enemy sends our way. These could be thoughts, temptations, and oppressions that innocently come into our mind. It all starts with our mind. The mind is a facilitator of the evil works of the flesh.

Romans 12:2, remember, tells us how to present ourselves: "Do not be conformed to this world, but be transformed by the renewing of your mind, that you may prove what the will of God is, that which is good and acceptable and perfect." When we turn our radio or television on, we have to realize what is coming into our mind. It is often a subtle message, and we need to be discerning. Spending time in the Word will help us to discern the things of this world.

Ephesians 6:17 says, "And take the helmet of salvation, and the sword of the Spirit, which is the word of God." That is not just your salvation experience but the *hope* of your salvation. This same phrase appears in 1 Thessalonians 5:8, where Paul says our helmet is the hope of our salvation: "But since we are of the day, let us be sober, having put on the breastplate of faith and love, and as a helmet, the hope of salvation." He is not talking about the hope that is built into salvation, which is our eternal life, but the confident expectation of our future in Christ. First John 3:3 says in effect, "If you have this hope within you, you will purify yourself." All the promises of Christ's coming keep our minds focused and therefore protected from the distractions around us.

The sword used here is the word *machaira*, the small sword that was worn on the soldier's side. If an enemy soldier breaks through the wall of shields, this is the sword to use against him. This is the one you use for hand-to-hand combat. I want you to know that the shield of faith and the sword of the spirit—the Word of God—have to work together. If you have not purposed in your heart to obey what Christ has said, then forget all the verses you have memorized because they are not going to do a thing to help you in warfare. The shield of faith becomes your willingness to obey the Word of God. That is the process for victory in spiritual warfare. It is faith, our intention to always obey God's Word, that gives life to the thoughts of God.

But if this shield is dropped, the thoughts of the world take root. You know when you are beginning to entertain a thought that you shouldn't. You simply need to stand firm and declare, "You are not going to get in. I have purposed in my heart to obey the things of God." That is the attitude you and I ought to have. It is not just your lifestyle committed to Christ, but it is also your deep desire to pray for other believers that they walk the same way. This is where we interlock our shield of faith with that of others.

In Ephesians 6:18 Paul continues: "With all prayer and petition pray at all times in the Spirit, and with this in view, be on the alert with all perseverance and petition for all the saints." Praying in the Spirit for the saints is what links our spiritual armor with theirs. So with our stand, our walk, our armor, and our prayer for one another, we can walk arm-in-arm and hand-and-hand. This brings glory to the Lord Jesus in the church.

The Power of God's Weapons

I was in Romania several years ago under Ceausescu's dictatorship with some other team members. It was a sad place to be. We stayed in different hotels so that no one would know who we were or that we were together. If we were stopped by the Secret Police we honestly could not tell them where anyone else in our party was because we didn't know. We didn't take Bibles except for our personal copies. One night in a hotel in Bucharest I became seriously ill with a high fever. I couldn't call home. I couldn't call anyone on the team because I didn't know where anybody was. I was totally on my own. Never in my life have I understood so well what it meant to walk by faith as I did that night. When Christ is all you have, that's the time you realize that Christ is all you need.

All I could do was pray. It was 1:10 A.M. on a Monday morning Romanian time, seven hours from Tennessee time. I prayed, "Lord, I don't know what to do. I'm afraid." My fever was climbing, I had no medicine, and because I had no water, I was becoming dehydrated. God reminded me that in five minutes Sunday night church would be starting back home in Tennessee. He said, "Hang on, in five minutes church starts at home, and I want to show you something." He didn't say that verbally, but it was impressed on my heart. At 1:18 in the morning my fever broke for no reason at all. I was able to sleep the rest of the night and travel over 400 miles the next day and continue to preach. I was sick during that time, but I progressively got better.

When I got home and was sharing that story in church, I had no idea what was going to happen. The choir began to weep, and they said, "Wayne, that Sunday night before church we were in choir practice and we couldn't go upstairs for the service because we were burdened that you were sick. We prayed that God would put His healing hand upon you."

I learned something that day. I learned what it means to pray in the Spirit. It does not mean that you pray in an unknown tongue or an ecstatic language. It means to be wearing the garment, living in the fullness of Christ, and letting all glory go to Him. God whispers in your ear the name of somebody and makes you a part of His plan. That's what praying in the Spirit means. It means being sensitive to the leadership of the Spirit. When I am sensitive to the Spirit, I am able to hear His prompting when He puts someone on my heart. I begin to pray as He directs me. I may not know until eternity comes how that warfare prayer impacted the person, but somehow it plays a role as God directs. He's the One who is leading.

I have never professed to know all the answers, but my encouragement to you is to be careful of the magic formulas that people give you regarding spiritual warfare. Remember, this is a hostile world, but the biggest enemy you have is not the devil and not the demons, but your fallen flesh. Your flesh has not gotten any more spiritual, and it is not going to get any more spiritual. Remember also that your flesh and your spirit are one person, and it is your spirit that quickens your flesh. You can't blame the devil—you must take responsibility for whatever happens.

Next time you're in a large bookstore, spend some time perusing some of the numerous books on warfare and weaponry. You'll find hundreds of pages and thousands of pictures of implements that mankind has invented to defend himself from other people. Then go home and reread Ephesians 6:10-18. The simplicity of the armor of God—truth, righteousness, peace, faith, salvation, the Word of God, prayer—will stand out in stark contrast to the weapons of fleshly warfare. By God's weapons alone will His kingdom come and His will be done, in earth as it is in heaven.

The Rest *of* Grace

13

Why We Never Arrive

Join me here on the back porch and let's talk together about the Christ life. We've tromped over biblical hill and dale for the last 12 chapters, surveying the landscape of the Christian life from almost every perspective. I trust you've been informed and encouraged. I trust you have a better grasp on the responsibility that is ours to allow the Christian life to become the Christ life.

What I've tried to say is that Christ is our life. He said it first, of course: "I am the way, and the truth, and the life" (John 14:6). But have we missed it along the way? Have we settled into the routines of Christianity to such a degree that we think we have become totally capable of doing it in our own strength? Think about your life. What parts of it do you know you absolutely could not accomplish without Christ?

In reality, we can accomplish none of it without Him. I don't mean we have to stop before taking a bite of a biscuit or a sip of iced tea to make sure we're doing it in Christ's strength. What I mean is this: In the areas of your life where temptation, conflict, and challenges occur, are you finding victory in Him? Are you finding that you're growing more in the sense that the spiritual life is not something you "have to do," but something you "get to do"? I hope so. Because once your eyes are opened to the pure pleasure and sweetness that comes from allowing Jesus of Nazareth to love others through you, life will never be the same.

I have said it over and over again in the pages of this book: We are just vessels through which Christ works. The Christ life is a journey. We will never arrive at a point where we don't have to struggle with our flesh anymore. Either the Lord will return or we will die before that ever happens. We don't have to live defeated lives, but we should expect struggles to come and go. In 2 Timothy 4:7 the apostle Paul says, "I have fought the good fight, I have finished the course, I have kept the faith." When he says, "I have fought the fight," I don't think he is referring to a battle with pagans or the world or the devil, but the battle with himself. All of us have a battle going on inside us.

The flesh wars against the Spirit and the Spirit against the flesh according to Galatians 5:17. Paul doesn't say the flesh wars against the Spirit when you are a young Christian and stops warring against it when you get older. As a matter of fact, I have found an intensification of the battles as I have gotten older. However, I've also found that the victory is much sweeter. The victory is much more easily achieved when my senses have been trained under righteousness because then I have an awareness of an ability that I didn't have before. But the battle still goes on.

The Normal Christian Life

Many people who preach the health-and-wealth gospel today would have passed out if they had emulated the apostle Paul. He suffered imprisonments, beatings, loneliness, boredom, coldness, and shipwreck. The man would never have been let into many of our churches today because he looked (and in fact was) homeless. When he asked Timothy to come to him he said, "Bring my coat and my books" (see 2 Timothy 4:13). I'm confident that those items probably represented the sum total of his possessions.

My word of encouragement to you if you find yourself in the midst of a struggle is, "Welcome to the normal Christian life." You ought to know by now what to do: Take it to the cross. If there is sin in your life, confess it. Don't listen to people who tell you that you don't need to confess it. Confess it and agree with God. Then appropriate the forgiveness that is already there for you. Not only that, but turn back to Him. Repentance is not saying, "God, I'm going to do better." I have never yet done better, and never will. And neither will you. Repentance is saying, "God, I'll do it Your way and depend upon You. I can't, but I'm going to let You be the strength to do this through my life."

Trust Him. The arrival point comes only when we see Jesus one day and have a glorified body. We will live and rule with Him forever. But for now we are on a journey. We are aliens in a strange country. We live in a hostile world. All the flesh wants to do is tear down what God's Spirit has built up. This book has been written to encourage you that it is not you but Christ in you. The results are not yours; they are His. Ministry hinges on this one truth: *Learn to appropriate Christ.* Then when you see Him one day, and He tests your works and rewards you for your faithfulness, you can rejoice and put your crowns back at His feet, and heaven will be even much sweeter because of what you've learned here.

Let me share with you how, even at my age, the battles never stop, but the victory gets more consistent in Jesus. Just a week ago in our church service my flesh raised its head—but Christ got the victory in my heart. My missions pastor, who loves Jesus as much as anybody on the face of this earth, got up and shared his heart. We were on a time schedule determined by television taping, and I knew I had 44 minutes to preach. He shared for almost 30 minutes, and I thought, "Oh, my goodness, he's ruining the schedule!" I began to get angry sitting there on the platform. Here I am, the one who preaches victory, who says that Jesus can be Jesus in your life, and I sat there fuming and almost missed what God was doing through my brother.

Before I could get up to preach I had to bow my heart before the Lord and say, "God, I'm wrong. I confess it to You. Your Spirit has convicted me. Lord, I realize once again the futility of ever thinking that the flesh is going to stop being addicted to sin." At that point, yielded to Him, I said, "Lord, I can't do this tonight. I'm aware of this now. You do it through me." The service was made much better because I was willing to surrender to Him.

The flesh never dies—that is for sure. But Jesus never leaves or forsakes us either. As long as He is faithful, we can have the victory. What happened to me in that church service will happen to you. You have to immediately reckon with the flesh. You have to say, "God, I'm putting my focus on You."

If I'm going to surrender to Him, the Word has to take priority in my life. I have to go to His Word with the problem I'm dealing with and say, "God, what do You say about it?" Then, recognizing that His Spirit lives within me, I need to make a choice to let the Holy Spirit do the changing. In the meantime, I have to take the responsibility of renewing my mind so it can be Christ in me and not me before Christ.

Blowing Up the Dams

I have a friend in Mississippi who owns a large stand of timber. When I was with him recently at his place in the country, he said, "Wayne, we are going to do something tremendous today. We are going to blow up beaver dams."

I said, "We are going to do what?"

"We are going to blow up beaver dams!"

"Why are we going to blow up beaver dams?"

"We raise trees. We have thousands of acres of swamp-land, but there are creeks and rivers that run through our land, and when the beavers get in there they dam up the rivers and the creeks, and the water backs up on the trees that we are trying to sell. If it sits on the trees for a certain period of time, it ruins the trees and we lose timber money. So we have to blow up the dams. First we have to trap the beavers, and then we have to blow up the dams. It's a weekly ritual if you're in the timber business."

"The beavers can rebuild the dams in a week?" I said. I couldn't believe it.

"Absolutely. You wouldn't believe how easily they can block the flow of a stream."

So the two of us got on a four-wheeler. I could just see Michael the archangel in heaven crying out, "Send ten legions of angels! Barber and his buddy are down there on a four-wheeler with a bag of dynamite. Hurry!"

So we got down in the swamp, and my friend got out in the water with his waders on and stuck two sticks of dynamite down into a beaver dam. I got behind a tree and he touched the two receptacles on the battery—and the result was awesome. The ground shook and the sky filled with debris. The water that moments before had looked almost stagnant started to move, slowly at first and then with a rush. You could almost sense the freedom in that water that had been dammed up but was now running pure and free again.

The following year I went back, and this time my friend had rigged up something that I thought certainly would bring the Marines in response: diesel fuel, fertilizer, and five sticks of dynamite to tackle a particularly large dam. Well, I've never experienced an explosion like that in my entire life. It was so big, it blew things 400 feet in the air. We went back to his house, which was a mile away, and when we pulled into his driveway, his son-in-law came out and asked, "What did you do?"

"Well, we just had a little explosion."

"A little explosion! Glasses fell over in the sink and broke. We were looking for cracks in the foundation of the house."

Blowing up dams is loud and it's fun. I guess it appeals to the "macho" side of men to go out and do stuff like that. But there's a lesson here. The water that was dammed up was meant to flow. The problem was that something had stopped it. Remember Jesus saying that out of you "shall flow rivers of living water" (John 7:38)? Perhaps the living waters of God's Holy Spirit have been dammed up in your life by sin or stubbornness. You are not allowing God to do what He wants to do in your life. You have stopped trusting (or maybe you've never begun trusting) that God says He will deliver you from sin and from all its consequences.

What I want you to understand is that when Scripture speaks of the power of God, it uses the word *dunamis*, from which we get our word "dynamite." Just as the dynamite on those beaver dams was sufficient to get the water flowing again, so God's power is sufficient to remove whatever is blocking the free flow of living water in you and me.

There is a song we sing that says,

> Would you be free from your burden of sin?
> There's pow'r in the blood, pow'r in the blood.
> Would you o'er evil a victory win?
> There's wonderful pow'r in the blood.

> There is pow'r, pow'r, wonder-working pow'r
> In the blood of the Lamb.
> There's pow'r, pow'r, wonder-working pow'r
> In the precious blood of the Lamb.

That Lamb is Jesus Christ.

If you will get before Him and confess your sin, and let the blood of Jesus cleanse you and turn your heart toward Him, living waters will flow from you. Let His Word renew your mind. He is already there. He is your sufficiency. He wants to live His life through you. The only barrier is you. When you are willing to allow Him to be everything He wants to be, you will find the life that you are looking for. It is Christ living His life through you. That is the Christ life!

Other Good
Harvest House Reading

HOW TO STUDY YOUR BIBLE
by *Kay Arthur*

Equips eager Bible students with tools that will help them to interact directly with Scripture itself. A dynamic, step-by-step guide on studying the Bible book by book, chapter by chapter, and verse by verse.

A PASSION FOR GOD
by *Greg Laurie*

The greatest commentary of Jesus' love and power is written in the words and actions of His people. Evangelist Greg Laurie explores the dynamic faith and experiences of the early church and discovers what these believers did to turn their world upside down. Discover how all believers are given the tools and courage to be bold witnesses for Christ, fueling the passion of faith in the world around them.

PATHWAY TO THE HEART OF GOD
by *Terry W. Glaspey*

Combining the wisdom of classical writers and thinkers of the faith with his own insightful, practical narrative, Terry Glaspey sheds light on the wonder and power of friendship with God. The words of C.S. Lewis, Martin Luther, Augustine, Corrie ten Boom, D.L. Moody, and a host of others reflect on the most compelling aspects of prayer.

Dear Reader,

We would appreciate hearing from you regarding this Harvest House non-fiction book. It will enable us to continue to give you the best in Christian publishing.

1. What most influenced you to purchase *The Rest of Grace?*
   - ❏ Author
   - ❏ Subject matter
   - ❏ Backcover copy
   - ❏ Recommendations
   - ❏ Cover/Title
   - ❏ Other_____

2. Where did you purchase this book?
   - ❏ Christian bookstore
   - ❏ General bookstore
   - ❏ Department store
   - ❏ Grocery store
   - ❏ Other_____

3. Your overall rating of this book?
   - ❏ Excellent ❏ Very good ❏ Good ❏ Fair ❏ Poor

4. How likely would you be to purchase other books by this author?
   - ❏ Very likely ❏ Not very likely ❏ Somewhat likely ❏ Not at all

5. What types of books most interest you? (Check all that apply.)
   - ❏ Women's Books
   - ❏ Marriage Books
   - ❏ Current Issues
   - ❏ Self Help/Psychology
   - ❏ Bible Studies
   - ❏ Fiction
   - ❏ Biographies
   - ❏ Children's Books
   - ❏ Youth Books
   - ❏ Other_____

6. Please check the box next to your age group.
   - ❏ Under 18 ❏ 18-24 ❏ 25-34 ❏ 35-44 ❏ 45-54 ❏ 55 and over

Mail to: Editorial Director
Harvest House Publishers
1075 Arrowsmith
Eugene, OR 97402

Name _____

Address _____

State _____ Zip _____

Thank you for helping us to help you in future publications!